The Promise-Powered Life *for Men*

How to See the Promises of God Fulfilled in Your Life

J. M. FARRO

Scripture quotations marked NIV are taken from THE HOLY BIBLE, NEW INTERNATIONAL VERSION®, NIV® Copyright © 1973, 1978, 1984, 2011 by Biblica, Inc.™ Used by permission. All rights reserved worldwide.

Scripture quotations marked AMP are taken from the Amplified Bible. Copyright © 1954, 1958, 1962, 1964, 1965, 1987 by The Lockman Foundation. Used by permission.

Scripture quotations marked NASB are taken from the NEW AMERICAN STANDARD BIBLE®. © Copyright 1960, 1962, 1963, 1968, 1971, 1972, 1973, 1975, 1977, 1995 by The Lockman Foundation. Used by permission.

Scripture quotations marked NKJV are taken from the New King James Version. Copyright © 1982 by Thomas Nelson, Inc. Used by permission. All rights reserved.

Scripture quotations marked MSG are taken from THE MESSAGE. Copyright (c) by Eugene H. Peterson 1993, 1994, 1995, 1996, 2000, 2001, 2002. Used by permission of NavPress Publishing Group.

Scripture quotations marked NLT are taken from the Holy Bible, New Living Translation. Copyright 1996, 2004. Used by permission of Tyndale House Publishers, Inc., Wheaton, Illinois 60189. All rights reserved.

Verses marked TLB are taken from The Living Bible. Copyright 1971. Used by permission of Tyndale House Publishers, Inc., Wheaton, Illinois 60189. All rights reserved.

Copyright © 2014 by J. M. FARRO
P.O. Box 434
Nazareth, PA 18064

Printed in the United States of America. All rights reserved under International Copyright Law. Contents and /or cover may not be reproduced in whole or in part in any form without the written consent of the Author.

ISBN-10: 1503256316

ISBN-13: 978-1503256316

Acknowledgements

I would like to take this opportunity to thank my husband, Joe, for helping me to put this project together, and for faithfully reading and editing my devotionals on a regular basis. I could not devote myself to my ministry work without his constant support and understanding. He has been my best friend and confidant for more than 40 years.

I also sincerely appreciate my son, Joseph, and all of the valuable technical support and computer help he has given me over the years. His expertise, confidence, and calmness in stressful times have been a great inspiration and encouragement to me.

A special thanks to my son, John, who has allowed me to serve on the staff of his extraordinary ministry, Jesusfreakhideout.com, for the past 16 years. I am ever so grateful to him for telling me those many years ago, "Mom, you should write some devotionals for my site..."

Cover Photo by Joseph DiBiase II

Introduction

When I got serious about my relationship with Christ more than twenty years ago, and began an in-depth study of the Scriptures, I discovered that I had inherited a wealth of promises from God Himself. I also discovered that these divine promises are not automatic. They have to be claimed and received by faith.

As I sought the Lord about receiving the full benefit of His promises, He showed me His instructions in Isaiah 62:6-7 (AMP): "You who [are His servants and by your prayers] put the Lord in remembrance [of His promises], keep not silence, and give Him no rest..." One of the best ways to activate the power and benefits of God's supernatural promises is to pray them back to the Lord. When we do this, we are in effect telling Him, "Lord, this is what You said, and I'm trusting You to keep Your Word."

Since I began making my prayers promise-centered, instead of problem-centered, I have seen my percentage of answered prayer increase dramatically. Why? Because when we pray God's promises, we are praying God's will. And the Bible says that "if we ask anything according to His will, He hears us," and we can be confident "that we have what we asked of Him". (1 John 5:14-15 NIV)

The Lord has given His children promises of provision, protection, power, deliverance, life, healing, strength, wisdom, peace, joy, victory, success, wholeness, freedom, and everything we need to live the abundant life in Christ, and to fulfill our God-given purpose and potential on this earth.

Scripture says that Jesus "carries out and fulfills all of God's promises, no matter how many of them there are". (2 Corinthians 1:20 TLB) I encourage you to dig into God's Word, asking the Lord to lead you to the promises that pertain to your specific needs. Believe them. Pray them. Claim them as your own. Then watch God go to work to prove His faithfulness every time!

Table of Contents

A GENTLE AND JUST GOD 1

DIVINE INTERVENTION AND PROTECTION 3

WINNING THE RESPECT OF OUTSIDERS 7

HE MAKES ALL THINGS NEW 11

COSTLY MISTAKES 15

PEACE FOR DECISIONS 19

DELAYS ARE NOT NECESSARILY DENIALS 23

OUR PEACE AND PERSONAL TIME WITH GOD 27

POWER FOR THE WEARY 31

THE PRICE OF A PASSIVE RESPONSE 33

CONSTRUCTIVE COMPLAINING 37

OUR HEART'S DESIRES 41

MAKING A DISTINCTION 45

CONFRONT PEOPLE DIRECTLY 49

VICTORY OVER TEMPTATION 53

REFUSING A FATALISTIC VIEW 57

BETTER TO TRUST THE LORD 61

OUR DREAMS OR HIS? 65

WHEN TROUBLE COMES 69

STRONGHOLDS OF HUMAN REASONING	73
I DESIRE TO DO YOUR WILL	79
REVENGE IS SWEET!	83
PRAYING FOR "SNAKES"	87
SUPERABUNDANTLY!	91
OUR TRUE STANDARD	95
BENEFITS AND BLESSINGS FROM GOD	99
DON'T MEASURE SHORT	103
EXPERIENCING GOD	107
DO THE RIGHT THING	111
PEOPLE ARE WATCHING	115
OUR SPIRITUAL MENTOR	119
THE QUESTION OF SUFFERING	123
NO PRESSURE!	127
WINNING BATTLES GOD'S WAY	131
THE BEST LESSON MY DAD EVER TAUGHT ME	135
THE HUMBLE GET THE HELP	139
SKILLS BLESSED BY GOD	143
SPIRITUAL SMOKESCREENS	145
GETTING BURNED	149
SMALL BEGINNINGS	153

REASONING AWAY HIS BLESSINGS	157
GOD'S ANTIDOTE FOR DISAPPOINTMENT	161
BATTLE SCARS	165
GIVE HIM REPEATED THANKS	169
WHEN WE 'MISS' GOD	171
THE REWARDS OF CHILDLIKE FAITH	175
SPEEDY ANSWERS	179
THE PROPER PERSPECTIVE	183
GIVING GOD CONTROL	187
LESSONS FROM JEHOSHAPHAT	191
ABOUT THE AUTHOR	195

A Gentle and Just God

"A bruised reed He will not break and a dimly burning wick He will not extinguish; He will faithfully bring forth justice." Isaiah 42:3 NASB

Here is a promise for you and me when we are at our weakest. This verse speaks of the coming Messiah, the Lord Jesus Christ, and Matthew rightly applies it to Him in his gospel. (Matthew 12:18-21) You see, God knew that there would be times when we would be so burdened by the cares of this world that we would feel bruised and battered – as though if we had to endure one more day of hardship and heartache, we would break. We might even feel as though we were no longer a shining light for Christ, but a dimly burning candle.

I felt this way myself not long ago, when I was laboring long and hard on a new ministry project, and it felt as though I was standing totally alone against the world, and the forces of darkness were coming against me. I was feeling so weak and weary at times that I would hear my thoughts saying things like, "Isn't this work my assignment from God? Why, then, am I continually facing delays and disappointments?"

As I spent time alone in God's presence and in His Word, He ministered to me through His promises. He reminded me that He will never kick me when I'm down, or let me fall apart. On the contrary, He will encourage me and strengthen me, and He will enable me to shine brighter than ever for His glory. And those who come against me when I am doing His will? God Himself will deal with them.

The New Living Translation of Isaiah 42:3 says: "He will not crush the weakest reed or put out a flickering candle. He will bring justice to all who have been wronged." If you are feeling weak and weary today, I have good news for you. You have a Savior who loves you enough to die for you, and He is ever ready to encourage you and lift you up, and to fight your battles for you!

Lord, I'm so thankful that even though You are a mighty and powerful God, You are also loving, gentle, and just. When I am feeling crushed or broken, remind me to turn to You first. Give me a trusting heart so that I will believe and act as though You truly care when I am hurting. Don't allow me to suffer in silence, but keep after me until I bring all my concerns and hurts to You. Today, I choose to look to You and cooperate with You, so You can minister hope and healing to me, and right all my wrongs!

Promise-Power Point: If I will turn to the Lord for help when I am feeling weak and bruised, He will deal gently with me and comfort me; He will fight my battles, and make me shine brighter than ever for His glory.

Divine Intervention and Protection

"Giving thanks is a sacrifice that truly honors Me. If you keep to My path, I will reveal to you the salvation of God." Psalm 50:23 NLT

When the hot water supply in our home began getting sporadic, my husband Joe and I knew that it was time to replace our electric hot water heater. It had been 13 years since Joe had installed our old water heater, so we weren't too surprised when we began having problems with it. The first thing I did was to pray that the Lord would provide us with the best unit at the best price. I had seen God lead us to extraordinary bargains before, so I asked Him to help us find a new water heater for the same price we paid for our old one. When Joe began researching new units, he discovered that they had doubled in price in the last 13 years. I told the Lord that I believed that He could still provide us with an exceptional deal. That's when Joe discovered an excellent new water heater that was half the price of the other new ones, and only a few dollars more than our old one. We had to special order our new heater because of the dimensions we needed. This meant that we would have to wait a few weeks for it to be delivered. During that time, our hot water supply diminished more and more every day, and I earnestly prayed that the Lord would not let it run out before the arrival of our new water heater. When the delivery was delayed even more than originally expected, I began thanking and praising God that we would not have to take any cold showers while we waited. The Lord graciously answered my prayers by making sure that we had at least lukewarm water right up until the time Joe was able to install our new hot water heater.

After this experience, the Lord revealed to me that one of the reasons that our hot water supply didn't quit on us, was because I had been in the habit of thanking and praising Him for it on a regular basis. Almost every time I take a shower, I try to remember to express my appreciation to God for hot water. I began doing this in recent years when He began teaching me that being grateful invites divine intervention and protection. As I thought about this, the Holy Spirit brought to my remembrance Psalm 50:23 (NLT), where God says, "Giving thanks is a sacrifice that truly honors Me. If you keep to My path, I will reveal to you the salvation of God." In this case, when the Lord says "salvation," He is referring to His saving acts on behalf of His devoted ones. You see, when we take our blessings for granted, we are at risk of losing them. We have to remember that the enemy of our souls, Satan, is always working to rob us of the good things of God. Jesus made this clear when He said that the devil "comes only to steal, kill, and destroy". (John 10:10) Expressing gratitude to God is actually a very powerful form of spiritual warfare. When we give repeated thanks to the Lord for the blessings He bestows, we actually form a hedge of protection around them, and we prepare the way for God to act on our behalf when they are threatened.

The NIV translation of this verse states, "He who sacrifices thank offerings honors Me, and he prepares the way so that I may show him the salvation of God." (Psalm 50:23 NIV) Our thanks and praise actually "prepare the way" for God to show Himself strong on our behalf when trouble comes. But we can't expect the same results when we haven't been in the habit of having an attitude of gratitude for our provision and blessings. If we are constantly grumbling because we don't have everything we want or need, then we are leaving the door open for the devil and his dark forces to plunder what we do have. Perhaps the car you have now is a sorry piece of machinery, and you desperately want a new one. Instead of complaining about it, thank God that you have it, and make your thanks sincere. Go ahead and pray for a new car if you need one, but do it with a grateful heart, and not a bitter or resentful one. By doing this, you are "preparing the way" for God to act on your behalf at the best possible time for you.

I guarantee that if you get into the habit of being thankful for what you have, the Lord will give you more and more to be thankful for. I encourage you to give thanks for the loved ones in your life, for your job, your house, your neighborhood, and your community. Give thanks for your car, your devices, appliances, utilities, and services. They might not be everything you want them to be, but in those cases, when you thank God for them, you really are offering a "sacrifice" of praise. As Scripture instructs us: "Therefore by [Jesus] let us continually offer the sacrifice of praise to God, that is, the fruit of our lips, giving thanks to His name." (Hebrews 13:15 NKJV) No matter what you are going through right now, I urge you to begin expressing your gratitude to the Lord for all of the good in your life. When you do, you will be creating a hedge of protection, and preparing the way for God to act mightily on your behalf in the days to come!

Lord, right now, I would like to thank and praise You for all of the blessings I enjoy every day. Forgive me for the times I have taken them for granted, and give me a new awareness of all the good in my life. Teach me how to lift my heart and voice to You in sincere gratitude each day. Remind me that doing this makes it difficult for the devil and his dark forces to steal from me. Thank You that as I give You Your heart's desires in this area, I will experience more blessings to express my gratitude for!

Promise-Power Point: When I live a life of praise and thanksgiving, I will see the salvation of God in extraordinary ways in times of trouble and need.

Winning the Respect of Outsiders

"Make it your ambition to lead a quiet life, to mind your own business and to work with your hands, just as we told you, so that your daily life may win the respect of outsiders and so that you will not be dependent on anybody." 1 Thessalonians 4:11-12 NIV

Hardly a day goes by that I don't pray these Scriptures for myself, my loved ones, and Christ followers everywhere. I believe that when we are living in accordance with these verses, God can use us to impact the lives of countless people while we are here on the earth.

The first thing the Lord instructs us to do here is to "make it [our] ambition to lead a quiet life". I can remember a time in my youth when I was living anything but a quiet life. I had just experienced the first real heartbreak of my young life, and I began going out every night after work. If I couldn't get a friend to go with me, I would go by myself. I wanted to be constantly surrounded by people and noise, in an effort to avoid dwelling on my pain, disappointment, and fear of the future. Quiet moments were the last thing I wanted to experience. What I didn't know then was that I was actually delaying my recovery and healing, instead of hastening it. If I had only stayed at home some evenings and sought God's comfort and strength, and His will for my life, I could have experienced the restoration and rewards that only He could give. Living a quiet life doesn't mean that we can't have any fun. On the contrary, it means being in the will of God, and living the blessing-filled life He has called us to.

The next thing the Lord tells us to do in this passage of Scripture is to "mind [our] own business". Years ago, when my extended family was going through some serious trials, I became so entangled in their affairs that it threatened my health and my sanity. I was a young wife and mother at the time, and I knew that I was not giving my husband and children the loving attention they deserved, as long as I was much too focused on the problems of others. After praying and doing some soul-searching, I finally told my relatives that from then on, they were to keep me updated only on a "need-to-know" basis. In other words, I didn't need to be involved in all of the behind-the-scenes nonsense going on among my family members. Did my new ground rules make some people angry and indignant? You bet they did. But I stood firm, and in the long run, it has saved me and my immediate family a world of hurt and harm. Trust me, there are things that you and I are better off not knowing, even where our loved ones are concerned. And if we seek the Lord about establishing boundaries and borders for our relationships, He will reward us with more joy and peace than we ever dreamed possible.

When the Scripture tells us to "work with [our] hands," it means that we should give our God-given assignments and responsibilities the best of our time and attention. Ephesians 2:10 (NIV) bears this out when it says: "For we are God's handiwork, created in Christ Jesus to do good works, which God prepared in advance for us to do." You and I have a job to do while we are still on this earth. That's one reason why, when we were saved, God didn't just take us up to heaven. He has "good works" for us to do here and now, and as we seek Him and His will for us daily, He will show us what they are, and He will equip and empower us to perform them with supernatural skill and energy. Keep in mind that your personal "ministry" could involve your duties as a parent, a child, a spouse, a neighbor, or an employee. Or, it could involve all those things. Once we get into the "flow" of serving where and how God wants us to, we will reap the material and spiritual rewards He has in store for us.

And what is the main goal of following the divine instructions that First Thessalonians 4:11-12 teaches? "So that [our] daily life may win the respect of outsiders." And "so that [we] will not be dependent on anybody." As we follow God's will in all of the areas mentioned here, we will experience the supernatural power, protection, and provision that will gain the respect of those who do not know the Lord, and we will position ourselves to influence and impact their lives for all eternity!

Lord, help me to live a quiet life, and to spend regular quiet times in Your presence and Your Word. Teach me how to mind my own business, and to establish boundaries for my life and my relationships that will enable me to live the Christ-centered, fruitful life that You've called me to. Reveal to me the works You want me to focus on at this time, and help me to perform them with supernatural skill and joy. Thank You that as I follow Your will and Your ways in these areas, I will "command the respect of the outside world, being dependent on nobody [self-supporting] and having need of nothing"! (1 Thessalonians 4:12 AMP)

Promise-Power Point: If I will lead the quiet life God has called me to, and if I will mind my own business and work with my hands according to His purposes for me, I will win the respect from others that will make me a world-changer for Christ.

He Makes All Things New

"Then He who sat on the throne said, 'Behold, I make all things new.'" Revelation 21:5 NKJV

When I heard that some friends of mine went through a harrowing and messy divorce, it grieved my heart. My husband and I had known this couple for close to 40 years, almost the whole time that Joe and I had been together. I couldn't shake the feelings of shock and discouragement after hearing the news, so I sought the Lord in prayer about it. "I don't get it, Lord. These friends of mine always seemed like the perfect couple. What happened?" As I listened intently for the Lord's answer, I sensed Him saying to my heart, "They forgot why they fell in love in the first place."

I knew very well what the Lord meant by those words. I had seen many couples over the years lose their appreciation for each other. And I had been guilty of the same mistake myself. It wasn't until my husband had a heart attack, and then open-heart surgery, that I realized just how much I had been taking him for granted. I asked God to forgive me for failing to cherish the wonderful man He had given me, and I asked Him what I could do to make it up to my husband. The Lord impressed upon my heart that He was prepared to renew my marriage, and to make it better than ever before, but that I was going to have to do my part. That's when He led me to begin meditating on how Joe and I met, and why we fell in love.

I started thinking about how Joe and I were in the same sociology class in college, and how our professor chose us to be in a skit together. Our assignment called for us to spend time with each other apart from the rest of the class, so we began talking, and Joe mentioned that he had a new car. When he asked if I'd like to see it, I said yes, and we ended up going out to lunch together. That led to us going to dinner that evening, and though I was usually a rather private person, I ended up telling Joe my entire life story. Before the evening ended, Joe announced, "I think I'll marry you!" I laughed when he said it, but his words warmed my heart, and drew me close to him.

The Lord was right. The more I thought about our "love story," the more my love and appreciation for my husband deepened, even though more than 40 years have passed since the day we met. And as I demonstrated newfound respect and admiration for Joe, it became clear that his love was deepening for me. In the Book of Revelation, Jesus says, "Behold, I make all things new." (Revelation 21:5 NKJV) I've discovered that the Lord is more than willing and able to make relationships and marriages new when we ask Him to, and when we agree to do our part in the process. I can't help thinking about all of the marriages that could have been saved if the husband and wife had only sought God's help, and had agreed to work with Him and each other.

Whether you have been married for a year or 40 years, or even more, I urge you to keep your own "love story" alive by keeping it in your thoughts, and allowing it to draw you closer to your spouse. Most of all, keep your marriage covered in prayer, and partner with the Lord for its protection. Then watch God do His part to bless it, and to make it new each and every day!

Lord, thank You for my spouse. Forgive me when I have taken her for granted, and when I've failed to treat her with the respect that she deserves. I ask that You renew our marriage, and make it better and stronger than before. Show us what our part is in the process, and help us to do it faithfully. Today, I commit to keeping our "love story" in my heart and mind every day!

Promise-Power Point: God is willing and able to make my marriage new again, as I demonstrate my willingness to do my part with His help.

Costly Mistakes

"In my prosperity I said, 'This is forever; nothing can stop me now! The Lord has shown me His favor. He has made me steady as a mountain.' Then, Lord, You turned Your face away from me and cut off Your river of blessings." Psalm 30:6-7 TLB

Not long ago, I heard from a man who had gone through a long period of trial and turmoil. He had been working in a distant country just to find a job to support himself and his wife, but when his company let him go, he fell into despair. He eagerly sought the Lord for His provision and guidance, and enjoyed the support and encouragement of godly friends. After a year of joblessness, he was blessed with a job in his home country, and several months later, he was promoted to an executive position. He and his wife rejoiced when the Lord blessed them with a baby girl. This man told of how their happiness faded when their baby contracted a serious illness, and he lost his job. He knew in his heart that his troubles were related to his lack of communication with the Lord during his successful years, and his pride over his personal accomplishments. He described how disappointed he was with himself, and he said that if he could turn back time, he would not make the same mistakes again. He asked me to pray that God would give him another chance to regain his career, and grant his child a complete recovery.

As I thought about this man's situation, I recalled King David's description of his own folly in Psalm 30, where he writes: "When I was prosperous, I said, 'Nothing can stop me now!' Your favor, O Lord, made me as secure as a mountain." (Psalm 30:6-7 NLT) David lost his focus. As he became more and more wealthy and successful, he began to focus more on his blessings and accomplishments, and less on the God who promoted and prospered him. David goes on to describe what happened when his foolishness resulted in the loss of God's favor. "Then You turned away from me, and I was shattered." (v. 7b) As the king realizes his mistake, he is heartbroken and despondent, and he wisely and humbly turns to the Lord. "I cried out to You, O Lord. I begged the Lord for mercy… Hear me, Lord, and have mercy on me. Help me, O Lord." (v. 8, 10) To his credit, David does not let his pride or foolishness stop him from admitting his mistakes to God, or seeking His mercy and restoration. We know that the Lord hears and answers David's pleas because the psalm concludes with, "You have turned my mourning into joyful dancing. You have taken away my clothes of mourning and clothed me with joy, that I might sing praises to You and not be silent. O Lord my God, I will give You thanks forever!" (Psalm 30:11-12 NLT)

In numerous places in the Bible, God warns His people against taking pride in their accomplishments and achievements at the expense of their relationship with Him. In Deuteronomy 8, Moses reminds the Israelites of how the Lord humbled them in the desert by causing them to rely on His provision. He tells them, "He did all this so you would never say to yourself, 'I have achieved this wealth with my own strength and energy.' Remember the Lord your God. He is the one who gives you power to be successful... But I assure you of this: If you ever forget the Lord your God…you will certainly be destroyed." (Deuteronomy 8:17-19 NLT) When we neglect the Lord, His ways, and His Word, we forfeit His divine protection and provision, and we make ourselves vulnerable to Satan's strategies to "steal, kill, and destroy" what we hold dear. (John 10:10)

The Bible reveals that God wants us to take these things to heart. As the Apostle Paul wrote: "All these things happened to them as examples – as object lessons to us – to warn us against doing the same things; they were written down so that we could read about them and learn from them…" And he issues this admonition: "So be careful. If you are thinking, 'Oh, I would never behave like that' – let this be a warning to you. For you too may fall into sin." (1 Corinthians 10:11-12 TLB) You and I must remain on guard at all times. We have an enemy who is dedicated to doing his level best to draw us away from God and His good plans and purposes for us, and it's absolutely imperative that we give the Lord first place in our lives in every respect. If you can identify with the man who wrote me, I urge you to turn to God in heartfelt repentance right now, and to seek His face and His favor. When you do, you will discover how eager He is to give you a fresh start and a new beginning!

Lord, I regret all the times that I have lived my life neglecting You, Your wisdom, and Your ways. Please give me a new opportunity to serve You with the wholehearted devotion You desire and deserve. Guard me from pride and self-sufficiency, and teach me how to live my life with a humble reliance upon You. Show me how to put You first in every area of my life so that I can enjoy all the protection and provision You reserve for Your faithful ones. Thank You that as I do my part, I will experience more victory and blessing than I have ever known!

Promise-Power Point: As the Lord rewards and promotes me for living a Christ-centered life, I will never forget that He is my true Source, but I will keep my focus on Him, and continue to enjoy an unhindered flow of His blessings.

Peace for Decisions

"Let the peace (soul harmony which comes) from Christ rule (act as umpire continually) in your hearts [deciding and settling with finality all questions that arise in your minds, in that peaceful state] to which as [members of Christ's] one body you were also called [to live]. And be thankful (appreciative), [giving praise to God always]." Colossians 3:15 AMP

When the huge in-the-wall air conditioner in our living room stopped working, my husband, Joe, and I had to decide what to do to replace it. Joe already had it in his mind that he wanted to buy a ductless split air unit. He had been researching them for many months, and he had heard from other people that split air units were the way to go. Joe continued to read information on websites. He watched countless videos about cooling options. And he talked to people who installed air conditioners for a living. Even so, after many months of failing to come to a decision, I finally told my husband that it was obvious that he did not have peace about investing in a split air unit, which might cost us more money than we could afford. I told Joe that perhaps his indecisiveness was a signal from God that we were heading in the wrong direction, and that we needed to redirect our thinking and our planning. We asked the Lord to show us what His best for us was in the situation, and we prayed that He would make us sensitive and obedient to His Spirit's leading in the matter.

I told Joe that we should at least explore the possibility of getting another in-the-wall air conditioner. But my husband insisted that he had already searched for one, and none could be found. I earnestly prayed that God would provide the perfectly-sized air conditioner for us, no matter what the odds were against it. And as we began searching anew, Joe was amazed when we discovered a new air conditioner that seemed to be only a bit larger than our old one. He warned me that he would have to make the hole in our living room wall larger, and that he would have to cut some of our vinyl siding on the outside of our home. He was preparing himself for a lot of work to make the new unit fit, but he finally gave in and ordered our new air conditioner. When it arrived, and our neighbors helped Joe to install our new appliance, everyone was amazed when it slid right into the hole that was already in our wall. That's when Joe and I looked at each other and smiled, knowing without a doubt that this was the Lord's best for us, and that we had made the right decision.

The Bible says: "Let the peace (soul harmony which comes) from Christ rule (act as umpire continually) in your hearts [deciding and settling with finality all questions that arise in your minds...]" (Colossians 3:15 AMP) This is the Scripture that I gave my husband when it became obvious to me that he had no peace about the initial option he had in mind for our air conditioner dilemma. I told him that very often, an absence of peace in a situation means that we are looking in the wrong place, or we are headed in the wrong direction, and that God has a different – and better – option for us. Confirmation of God's best often comes when we change direction, and then everything falls into place. That is literally what happened when we put our new air conditioner into the hole in our living room wall. That's not to say that we won't encounter any obstacles when we head down the path the Lord has chosen for us. After all, Satan, the enemy of our souls, does not want us in the perfect will of God, and he is likely to try to get us off course. But it means that there will be a Holy Spirit "flow" present when we are headed in the right direction. And even if a part of us is anxious or fearful, we will have a deep-down sense of peace that we are in the perfect will of God.

If you are in a relationship right now, and you don't have peace about it, that absence of peace may be God's way of warning you to leave that person behind. Or perhaps you are planning on making a large purchase that you have an unsettled feeling about. God could be telling you to pause and pray for fresh revelation from Him in the matter. Or maybe you are experiencing health problems, and the course of healing that you have chosen has left you feeling uneasy. Whatever you don't have peace about today, I urge you to seek God's will once again in the matter, even if you have done so in the past. Nothing would be sadder than for you to end up settling for less than God's absolute best, especially when you don't have to.

Lord, I come to You today to seek Your wisdom, Your direction, and Your guidance for my life. Grant me divine discernment and insight that will help me to see things from Your perspective, and to take the course of action that is Your perfect will for me. Give me fresh revelation from heaven that will lead me in the way of peace for every area of my life. Thank You that as I follow Your peace, and choose Your will above my own, I will receive the provision, the healing, and the relationships that are Your best for me!

Promise-Power Point: As a follower of Christ, I can know and perform God's will when I seek Him and His wisdom in every situation, and be sensitive and obedient to His perfect leading.

Delays are Not Necessarily Denials

"However, when the Son of Man comes, will He find [persistence in] faith on the earth?" Luke 18:8 AMP

When my brother-in-law, John, was having problems with his laptop, my husband, Joe, offered to work on it for him. Joe spent a lot of time on the project, and then he packaged the computer up and mailed it back to his brother, who lives hundreds of miles away. He called his brother regularly, asking if he received the laptop, but days turned into weeks with no sign of the machine. My brother-in-law was convinced that he would never see his laptop again, and my husband began to feel guilty about not spending the money to insure it. It seemed like everyone had given up on that package – except me. I remember praying numerous times: "Lord, I know that even now, You can lead that laptop safely back to Joe's brother, and I'm asking You to do that because nothing is impossible with You!" Exactly two months later, my husband got a call from his brother, saying that his package had been sitting in his local post office the entire time, but no one had ever notified him of its arrival!

This experience made me think of Jesus' parable of the persistent widow in Luke 18. It's a powerful passage that begins with the verse: "One day Jesus told His disciples a story to illustrate their need for constant prayer, and to show them that they must keep praying until the answer comes." (Luke 18:1 TLB) It's a lesson that calls us to persevere in prayer for those things that God puts on our heart. And Jesus ends it by issuing us a challenge: "However, when the Son of Man comes, will He find [persistence in] faith on the earth?" (Luke 18:8 AMP) I could have easily talked myself out of praying for the Lord to restore that laptop, and for a while, I did. I told myself that by refusing to pay for the mailing insurance, my husband was being careless and cheap, and God wanted to teach him a lesson by its failing to reach its destination. But then I decided to give God the opportunity to do something unexpected, so I persevered in prayer. It made all the difference. How many times do we talk ourselves out of blessings and rewards by telling ourselves that we don't deserve them, or that perhaps it's not God's will for us? What would happen if we began to believe and act as though God wants to bless us even when we don't deserve it, as long as our hearts are bent toward Him? First of all, we would believe Him for greater things. And secondly, we wouldn't stop praying for His blessings until they came to pass in our lives.

One thing that we forget too easily is that God likes to work behind the scenes. Scripture even says, "Clearly, You are a God who works behind the scenes." (Isaiah 45:15 MSG) Just because we don't see any evidence with our eyes that God is working in a situation, that does NOT mean that He is not working. The prophet Isaiah said of the coming Messiah, "He will not judge by what he sees with his eyes or decide by what he hears with his ears." (Isaiah 11:3 NIV) Christ Himself instructs us to, "Stop judging by mere appearances and make a right judgment." (John 7:24 NIV) If we judge God's activities on this earth only through our five senses, we will walk in error as much as the rest of the world, and we will not operate in the supernatural, as the Lord calls us to. We have to believe that as long as we are praying and believing, God is busy working behind the scenes on our behalf.

It has been rightly said that with God, "Delays are not necessarily denials." There are many times when we ask the Lord for something and He is not saying "no," but "wait". That means that the answer is on its way, IF we continue to stand in faith until the thing God challenged us to believe Him for comes to pass. Sometimes, we won't know for a very long time if what we are praying for is actually God's will. That is one of the reasons why we have to practice becoming more sensitive to the Holy Spirit's leading. Quitting before we receive the answer that God desires for us can be a greater sin than persisting in prayer for something that is not His will. What is the Lord challenging you to believe Him for today?

Lord, forgive me for the times that I failed to persevere in prayer when You wanted me to. Help me to become more attuned to Your Spirit's leading by spending regular time alone with you – praying, reading Your Word, and listening for Your voice. Remind me often that You are a God who works behind the scenes. Thank You that my persistence in prayer will open the door for You to do new and mighty things in my life!

Promise-Power Point: I will not fail to receive the blessings, plans, and opportunities that the Lord has for me when I determine to become sensitive to His leading, and persistent in my prayers.

Our Peace and Personal Time with God

"I will listen to what God the LORD says; He promises peace to His people, His faithful servants – but let them not turn to folly." Psalm 85:8 NIV

I once heard a godly man say that when we neglect our personal time with God, our burdens become unbearable. I discovered for myself just how true this is recently when I began spending less time with the Lord and His Word each morning. At first, I didn't even realize what I was doing, and then when I began to suspect it, I chose to ignore it. I suppose that I inwardly gave myself permission to get a bit "sloppy" in this area, thinking that no harm would be done. But then the Lord showed me Psalm 85:8 (NIV), which says, "I will listen to what God the LORD says; He promises peace to His people, His faithful servants – but let them not turn to folly." What is folly? It's basically a costly lack of good sense or judgment. The Lord was warning me here that while He has promised me peace because of my devotion to Christ, I would not be able to reap the full benefit of His promise as long as I was neglecting my personal time with Him.

One of the requests I have heard most from people I have come in contact with through my ministry all these years is, "Please pray that I will discipline myself to spend private time with the Lord each day." These people have undoubtedly been convicted by the Holy

Spirit as I was when I let my time with God slip. They were not enjoying the peace that Jesus promised His faithful followers when He said, "I am leaving you with a gift – peace of mind and heart. And the peace I give is a gift the world cannot give. So don't be troubled or afraid." (John 14:27 NLT) As a result, the wear and tear of daily life was pressing upon them.

Think about the people you love most in this world, and how much you love spending time with them. You know that you can't have a truly personal, intimate, growing relationship with a loved one unless you spend quality time with them on a regular basis. It's the same with God. We simply cannot expect to have the same kind of relationship with the Lord when we neglect our quiet times with Him, as we would have if we made spending time with Him our highest priority. And our level of intimacy with God will have a tremendous impact on our level of peace. The apostle Peter wrote: "Grace and peace be multiplied to you in the knowledge of God and of Jesus our Lord." (2 Peter 1:2 NASB) It's a scriptural truth that we receive more and more divine favor, power, and peace as we spend quality time with the Lord. The Living Bible puts it this way: "Do you want more and more of God's kindness and peace? Then learn to know him better and better." (2 Peter 1:2 TLB) And one of the best ways to get to know the Lord better is to give Him our undivided attention each day in prayer and Bible reading, since the Scriptures are filled with the truths of God.

We live in a very busy, hectic, and noisy world filled with people and circumstances that will crush us if we let them. Before Jesus went to the cross, He spoke words of comfort and reassurance to His disciples, telling them: "I have told you all this so that you will have peace of heart and mind. Here on earth you will have many trials and sorrows; but cheer up, for I have overcome the world." (John 16:33 TLB) Because Christ overcame the world, those who choose to follow Him can be overcomers, too. But only when we have the "peace of heart and mind" that He promises – the peace that we forfeit when we neglect our personal time with Him. If you have been lacking peace in your life lately, could it be that you have been putting other things or people ahead of your relationship with God?

Lord, I thank You for Your promise of peace to Your faithful ones. I know that no matter what is going on in my life, You are able to sustain me with Your own special kind of peace. Please help me to cooperate with You each day so that the troubles and trials of this world will not disillusion, discourage, or depress me. Help me to discipline myself to spend quality time with You each day in undistracted and unhurried prayer, Bible reading, and meditation. Thank You that as I follow Your lead in this area, You will fill me with Your unshakable, supernatural peace of mind and heart!

Promise-Powered Point: As a devoted follower of Christ, I can receive and enjoy the peace that only the Prince of Peace Himself can give, when I invest the time and effort to get to know Him better and better.

Power for the Weary

"Let the weak say, I am strong [a warrior]!" Joel 3:10 AMP

The other day, my husband, Joe, spent the entire afternoon outdoors cleaning our duck pond, mowing the lawn, and tidying up our shed. When he came back indoors, he exclaimed, "I'm exhausted and can hardly move!" I had been cleaning house all day myself, so I had a pretty good idea of how he felt. Nevertheless, I told my husband that Scripture tells us, "Let the weak say, 'I am strong.'" (Joel 3:10 NKJV) Joe laughed it off, but I told him that if he continued to voice his exhaustion and weakness – guess what? – he was going to feel more and more tired all the time, and he wouldn't be able to accomplish anything for the rest of the day.

The prophet Isaiah received some startling revelation on this subject that has been encouraging God's people for centuries. He wrote: "[The Lord] gives power to those who are tired and worn out; He offers strength to the weak." (Isaiah 40:29 NLT) When you and I have reached our apparent limits, we can remind ourselves that God offers us His supernatural power and strength. But we often have to ask Him for it, and receive it by faith. We can simply say: "Lord, I'm feeling tired, weary, and worn out right now. But I thank You for Your offer to revive me. I ask that You fill me afresh with Your power and Your strength. I believe I receive them right now, Lord, and I give You all the praise, in Jesus' name!" Then, go about your business, and declare with confidence, "I am strong in the Lord!" (Ephesians 6:10)

With the Holy Spirit dwelling in you and me, and with God's Word and promises stored in our hearts, we have access to heavenly resources in trying times that will enable us to live fruitful, productive, and energetic lives. Don't settle for less than God's very best in this area. Rise up and walk in the strength and victory that belong to you in Christ!

Lord, when I am feeling weak and worn out, help me to look to You to revive, refresh, and energize me. Don't let me live a mediocre and defeated life when You have promised to supply everything I need to live the abundant life Jesus died to give me. Remind me to spend time feeding on Your Word each day so that I can be infused with supernatural power to accomplish all that You have called me to. Thank You that as I continually depend on You for wisdom and strength, I will fulfill my God-given purpose and potential in this world!

Promise-Powered Point: *As a follower of Christ, I have heavenly resources at my disposal, so when I feel weak, tired, or depleted, I can experience the uplifting power of God in every fiber of my being, as I claim His promise of strength in faith.*

The Price of a Passive Response

"The righteous face many troubles, but the Lord rescues them from each and every one." Psalm 34:19 NLT

My paternal grandmother lived with me and my family the entire time I was growing up. She was a woman of faith, and she taught me my first prayers. Unfortunately, I didn't discover how many of her beliefs were unscriptural until I began studying the Scriptures many years later. For instance, one saying of hers was, "Once you get something, it never goes away." She was speaking of bodily ailments, and as she got older and had more and more health problems, she truly believed that she would have them for the rest of her days. And she usually did.

When I began studying the Bible in-depth, along with Christ's teachings, I discovered that having a passive attitude like my grandmother's can get us out of the will of God and keep us from His best. Every day, in every situation, God says to His people: "Today I have given you the choice between life and death, between blessings and curses. I call on heaven and earth to witness the choice you make. Oh, that you would choose life, that you and your descendants might live!" (Deuteronomy 30:19 NLT) Notice that the Lord didn't say, "Now that you have chosen to follow Me, you will automatically receive life and blessing in every situation." No, that's simply not how it works. Why? Because there are opposing forces in this world that don't want you and me to be blessed, healthy, and successful. Jesus said: "The thief comes only to steal and kill and destroy; I came that they may have life, and have it abundantly."(John 10:10 NASB) The Son of God wants to minister the life of God to us, while the devil wants to minister death. It's our responsibility to choose life over death in all things, even where the health of our bodies is concerned.

Some Christians are quick to surrender to every bodily affliction that comes their way. Some even suspect that it's God who is making them suffer. The problem with this kind of thinking is that if we view our afflictions as from the Lord, wouldn't it then be a sin for us to go to the doctor – or to take medicine – to try to gain some relief? And wouldn't it be offensive to God for us to pray for our healing? It's true that we live in a fallen world, and that there are consequences to sin, which could cause some ailments in these fleshly bodies of ours. But it's also true that as Christ-followers, we have the privilege – and even the obligation – to pray and believe God for good things while we are still here on earth. Why else would Jesus tell us to continually "ask, seek, and knock" so that we could live the abundant life He died to give us? (Matthew 7:7-11) As Romans 8:31-32 (NLT) says: "What shall we say about such wonderful things as these? If God is for us, who can ever be against us? Since He did not spare even His own Son but gave Him up for us all, won't He also give us everything else?"

One of the most inspiring testimonies in the Bible is the account of King Hezekiah in Second Kings 20:1-7 (NKJV). Here, the good king is on his sickbed, and God Himself tells the prophet Isaiah to go to Hezekiah and tell him to get his house in order because he is going to die of his affliction. What is the king's response? He turns to the Lord in prayer, pleading for His mercy. And as a result, God tells him, "I have heard your prayer, I have seen your tears; surely I will heal you. And I will add to your days fifteen years." (verses 5 & 6) Suppose Hezekiah had adopted my grandmother's passive attitude? He would have missed out on a miracle that is inspiring lives thousands of years later.

When trouble of any kind comes our way, we can actively "choose life" by praying and believing God for good things, and claiming His promises of healing, provision, and deliverance. One promise that I pray and stand on every single day for myself and my loved ones is Psalm 34:17 (AMP): "When the righteous cry for help, the Lord hears, and delivers them out of all their distress and troubles." I refuse to take a passive stance against distressing situations that come against me and my family, and I make it my business to seek God for His wisdom, assistance, and power – trusting Him to keep His Word. What have you been passively accepting lately that the Lord might want you to refuse and resist?

Lord, Your Word says that "every good and perfect gift" is from You, so please remind me of that whenever adversity comes my way. (James 1:17) I know that You can bring great good out of even the worst circumstances (Romans 8:28), but help me not to adopt a passive attitude when it's Your will for me to stand against attacks on my body, my marriage, my family, or my finances. Teach me how to "submit" to You and "resist the devil" in every situation. (James 4:7) Thank You that as I am sensitive and obedient to Your Spirit's leading in these areas, I will never miss out on Your very best!

Promise-Powered Point:** **When trouble comes my way, I will refuse to take a passive posture, and I will actively seek the Lord's wisdom and will in prayer, fighting the good fight of faith with His Word and His promises.

Constructive Complaining

"Not by might, nor by power, but by My Spirit, says the Lord Almighty – you will succeed because of My Spirit, though you are few and weak." Zechariah 4:6 TLB

Sometimes, on days when I am at my son, John's, house taking care of my grandson, William, I will pick up lunch for us, and then drop by a coffee shop to buy beverages and a treat or two. Last winter, which was especially harsh here in Eastern Pennsylvania, the driveway of the drive-up window at this restaurant suffered a huge pothole that was impossible to avoid. For weeks, I drove through that driveway and prayed that the Lord would send someone to repair that hole, but nothing changed. Then one day, the people working at the drive-up window completely botched up my order. I was so disgusted that I filled out an online survey for the coffee shop, and I described in detail how my order was ruined. I also included a complaint about the huge pothole in their drive-thru driveway. The next day, I was surprised when the owner of the restaurant called me and apologized profusely for the poor service I had received the day before. And I was completely stunned the next time I went to that coffee shop. Not only was the drive-thru pothole completely repaired, but the entire parking lot was beautifully paved.

Too often, we have a tendency to sit back and wait for someone else to complain about something that we know is wrong. We will gripe about the sorry condition of something, or shabby service, and then say to ourselves, "Surely someone will complain about this!" But many times, God is waiting for US to do the hard work of confronting and complaining. When we do, He will back up our complaint with divine intervention and action to support our efforts.

Scripture says, "Not by might, nor by power, but by My Spirit, says the Lord Almighty – you will succeed because of My Spirit, though you are few and weak." (Zechariah 4:6 TLB) This is the Lord's promise to His people that when the odds are stacked against us, and we are few in number and without apparent resources, the Spirit of God will intervene and fight our battles for us. But there is usually a part for us to play in this process. Undoubtedly, we will have to seek the Lord in earnest prayer, sometimes many times. And if we ask Him to, God will show us who we need to confront, and perhaps lodge a complaint against. When we do our part, we can rest assured that the Lord will be faithful to do His. Oftentimes, part of God's job is to turn, direct, or change the hearts of others. The Bible says, "The king's heart is like channels of water in the hand of the Lord; He turns it wherever He wishes." (Proverbs 21:1 NASB) If God can turn the hearts of kings, don't you think He can direct the heart of a coffee shop owner? You bet He can.

If you and I are going to impact this world for Christ, then we must get a revelation of how powerful our prayers can be. The apostle James wrote, "The earnest prayer of a righteous person has great power and produces wonderful results." (James 5:16 NLT) Our prayers will PRODUCE! Through the power of God, they can produce salvation, healing, deliverance, and provision. They can produce divine protection in the most dangerous circumstances. The devil would like nothing better than to have you think that your prayers couldn't possibly make a difference in someone's life, or in an "impossible" situation. If you believe his lies, then even though your prayers have the potential to change lives and circumstances, they will remain weak and ineffective because of your unbelief. Don't be fooled!

In every situation, there is a right way and a wrong way to complain. Our complaints should always be constructive, not destructive. We are called to "speak the truth in love" because we belong to Christ. (Ephesians 4:15 NLT) Scripture tells us, "And whatever you do or say, let it be as a representative of the Lord Jesus, all the while giving thanks through Him to God the Father." (Colossians 3:17 NLT) Remember who you are representing when you lodge a complaint. When you do it in a manner that pleases the Lord, He will get involved, and a favorable outcome will result. Can you think of a situation that needs this kind of attention from you today?

Lord, Your Word says that You make me bold as a lion for Your glory. (Proverbs 28:1) Show me what people and situations I need to confront and complain about as I go about my daily life. I regret all the times I allowed fear or a lack of confidence to keep me from doing Your will. When I am tempted to shy away from following Your lead in this area, remind me of Your promise to intervene and back me up as I take steps to obey You. Remind me of how powerful and effective my prayers can be because I belong to You. Thank You that as I believe Your Word and act upon it, lives and situations will be changed for Your glory!

Promise-Power Point: It doesn't matter if the odds are stacked against me; when God calls me to confront or complain, all of my efforts will succeed when I confidently and prayerfully step out in faith, and expect Him to strengthen and support me.

Our Heart's Desires

"Delight yourself in the Lord and He will give you the desires of your heart." Psalm 37:4 NIV

Since I've been walking closely with the Lord these past 20+ years, I have discovered time and time again how He loves to give us the desires of our hearts. When my 22-year-old car began breaking down in the worst possible places, I began pleading with the Lord to provide me with a more reliable one. He answered that prayer by causing my husband, Joe, to offer me his newer car. For the next two years, Joe drove that old vehicle to work every day without complaint, even though he had to endure a constant stream of ridicule from his coworkers.

When it was time to retire our old car for good, Joe began shopping for a new one. He did his homework and went to the auto dealership knowing exactly what he could afford, and what he wanted. The first time he called me from the dealership, he told me that he had driven the car he thought he wanted. When he described it, my heart sank. I had been believing God for three years for a particular car that was bigger and more stylish than the one that Joe was considering. I asked the Lord to intervene and make sure that Joe made the right choice. And I encouraged Joe to do the same, and to even consider waiting until the following day to make a decision.

I continued to pray that the Lord would not allow us to make a purchase that we would regret later on. And I asked Him to shut every door against our buying the wrong car. I also reminded God about the car that I had been believing Him for all along, knowing that He is often the One who puts certain desires in our hearts in the first place. I've discovered that He does this so that we can partner with Him to receive His best. The next day, when Joe went back to the dealership, he found out that the car he drove the previous day, and all those like it, had been sold. He was sorely disappointed, and I tried to encourage him, saying that God must have had something better in mind for us. I earnestly prayed for God's favor upon my husband, and as it turned out, the dealership offered Joe the bigger, more stylish car that I wanted, for less money than the smaller one! Joe and I both knew that this was God's best for us, and now every time I get in that car with my husband, I thank and praise the Lord for giving me the desire of my heart – at an extraordinary price!

Perhaps you have a desire in your heart right now that seems out of reach for you. If you are living for the Lord, and finding your delight in Him, you don't have to settle for less than His very best. Ask Him for the desires of your heart today, believing with all your heart that He's a good God, and He loves to bless you abundantly!

Lord, teach me how to make You the delight of my life. Expand my vision so that I can believe You for the extraordinary things You have in store for me. Help me to never settle for less than Your best. And align my will with Yours so that I'll only have desires that please You. Today, I choose to cooperate with You to receive all the too-good-to-be-true blessings You have for me!

Promise-Power Point: When I live my life loving the Lord and delighting in Him, He will give me the desires of my heart, no matter how unlikely they may seem.

Making a Distinction

"So Moses stretched out his hand toward heaven, and there was thick darkness in all the land of Egypt three days. They did not see one another; nor did anyone rise from his place for three days. But all the children of Israel had light in their dwellings." Exodus 10:22-23 NKJV

When my husband, Joe, was going through some tough times where his career and his job situation were concerned, I earnestly prayed that the Lord would send him some special encouragement. One evening, he was meeting with some friends and business associates at a restaurant near his workplace. Just as Joe and his companions were finishing their dinner and ordering dessert and coffee, a severe thunderstorm swept through the area and knocked out all the power. As darkness fell upon the entire restaurant, the emergency lighting kicked on. It happened to be located right above the table where my husband was sitting. Joe's waiter came by and declared to him and his dining companions, "You are the only ones with light in the whole place! Even the kitchen crew is in darkness!"

When my husband arrived home that evening and told me about his experience, his amazement was evident upon his face. I suddenly recalled the Scripture in Exodus, which says, "But all the children of Israel had light in their dwellings". (Exodus 10:23 NKJV) It was an illustration of how the Lord often chooses to make a distinction between those who love and serve Him, and those who do not. Don't you think that the hearts of the Israelites were encouraged by God's demonstration of power and favor on their behalf? You bet they were. And so was my husband's heart encouraged that night at the restaurant. I confess that I spend a lot of time praying for encouragement for myself, my loved ones, and others. Being encouraged in difficult times can make the difference between success and failure, and victory and defeat, because we can be tempted to give up when we are under intense pressure. Causing us to stand out in a crowd is one way the Lord can bring encouragement.

Making a distinction between God's people and the rest of the world is a common theme throughout Scripture. Psalm 91:7-8 (NIV) says: "A thousand may fall at your side, ten thousand at your right hand, but it will not come near you. You will only observe with your eyes and see the punishment of the wicked." We have all heard testimonies of how the Lord protected His people in the midst of disaster and calamity. Meditating on promises like these can give us the faith and courage to pray for divine protection and safety for ourselves and our loved ones. Psalm 37:19 (NIV) says: "In times of disaster they will not wither; in days of famine they will enjoy plenty." Here, the Lord promises His people supernatural strength and provision in the hardest of times.

I believe that there are many times when it is entirely scriptural to ask God to make a distinction between His people and the rest of the world – whether it's on our own behalf, or for the sake of His other saints. Malachi 3:18 (NIV) says: "You will again see the distinction between the righteous and the wicked, between those who serve God and those who do not." I have put this verse in prayer form, and have prayed it for myself and others, inviting the Lord to reveal His power and favor in the lives of His people. We can pray a prayer like this with confidence, as long as we do so with a right heart. Scripture says, "Even in darkness light dawns for the upright, for the gracious and compassionate and righteous man." (Psalm 112:4 NIV) God fulfilled this promise on my husband's behalf in a literal sense that night in the restaurant when the lights went out. But there is an even greater divine message behind this promise for every one of us – that even in our darkest times, God's light will come shining through!

Lord, I thank You that it is Your desire to make a distinction between Your people and the world, when it glorifies You. Guide me by Your Spirit so that I may know when to pray for You to do exactly that. Give me a revelation of how precious in Your sight Your chosen ones are. Thank You for making me stand out in a crowd in ways that will draw others to You!

Promise-Power Point: I will witness the Lord making a distinction between myself and others when I need encouragement and reassurance to persevere in doing His will.

Confront People Directly

"Do not nurse hatred in your heart for any of your relatives. Confront people directly so you will not be held guilty for their sin." Leviticus 19:17 NLT

I heard from a dear lady recently who said that she was having trouble getting along with people. She lamented the fact that every time a relationship of hers became one-sided, and she would attempt to confront the person and tell them frankly how they were making her feel mistreated and used, they would react with anger, indignation, or spitefulness. In some cases, they would even cut her off, leaving her feeling even more alone than she already did. She suspected that part of the problem was that people simply didn't like being confronted, even when the confronter did their best to be tactful and diplomatic. She asked for prayer and advice, because she desperately wanted to please the Lord with her relationships, but she wasn't exactly sure how to do that.

I told this dear woman that there are times when we simply cannot "pray away" relationship problems, and God expects us to deal with them directly. The Bible says that Christians are to "speak the truth in love." (Ephesians 4:15 NLT) And this principle applies even when confronting people lovingly causes them to react badly. Very few people like being corrected, or told that their behavior is unacceptable, but the fact is that all of us have a tendency to be selfish and self-centered. Because of that, God requires us to establish wise and healthy boundaries and limits for our lives, so that the people we are in relationship with won't think that they can control us or take advantage of us.

We can live our entire lives trying to avoid confronting people that need to be confronted, but all we are doing is giving these folks permission to oppress us, and to keep us from obeying the Lord and fulfilling the call of God on our lives. Then we will always carry around resentment in our hearts toward these people, and ALL of our relationships will be poisoned. We will end up sacrificing our sanity and our God-given purpose and potential, because we will be focusing on trying to keep these folks happy. And in the long run, it will all be in vain because God will not bless or protect these toxic relationships.

What is the solution to this madness? We must confront those people who the Lord leads us to confront, leaving the consequences of our obedience in God's hands. If you are not used to dealing with people's wrong behavior, then let me warn you that you are going to experience some serious feelings of guilt. But that is actually a positive response in these cases. It means that you are growing and making progress in establishing healthy boundaries for your relationships and your life, and eventually, you will reap the rewards that God has in store for you.

The Bible says: "Do not nurse hatred in your heart for any of your relatives. Confront people directly so you will not be held guilty for their sin." (Leviticus 19:17 NLT) This principle applies to all of our relationships – in our homes, our neighborhoods, our workplaces, our schools, and everywhere else. If we fail to "confront people directly" about their wrongdoing, then we will not only harbor resentment for them in our hearts, but we will suffer the consequences of our disobedience before God. I especially like how the Message Bible puts it: "Don't secretly hate your neighbor. If you have something against him, get it out into the open; otherwise you are an accomplice in his guilt." (Leviticus 19:17 MSG) Many times, doing the hard work of confronting others can result in clearing the air, and clearing the way to deeper and more satisfying relationships. One thing is for certain – if we refuse to deal with those people who the Lord expects us to deal with, we will be choosing to multiply our own misery, and to totally miss out on a chance for that relationship to ever improve.

Scripture promises: "Whoever rebukes a person will in the end gain favor rather than one who has a flattering tongue." (Proverbs 28:23 NIV) Even if the people we confront don't initially take our frankness very well, in the long run, they are likely to respect us for it. And even if they don't, we will gain the favor of God, and reap the rewards He promises. Who is it that the Lord is prompting you to deal with today?

Lord, fill me with a holy boldness to "confront others directly," instead of nursing a grudge against them in my heart. When I am tempted to shy away from dealing with others the way You want me to, remind me of how I will suffer for it in the long run. When someone reacts badly to my attempts to confront them according to Your will, please comfort me and reassure me that I did the right thing. Help me to continually seek Your will and Your wisdom for all of my relationships. Thank You that as I follow Your lead, I will reap the untold rewards that can only come from You!

Promise-Powered Point: As a Christ-follower, I am equipped with everything I need to resist resentment toward others, and to deal with them directly and honestly for their good, for my good, and for the glory of God.

Victory Over Temptation

"In the day when I called, You answered me; and You strengthened me with strength (might and inflexibility to temptation) in my inner self." Psalm 138:3 AMP

If you have trusted Christ as your personal Savior, you are eternally saved and on your way to heaven. But while you are in this world, you have a formidable enemy named Satan who seeks to destroy your witness for Christ, and keep you from fulfilling your God-given purpose. The Bible says: "Be self-controlled and alert. Your enemy the devil prowls around like a roaring lion looking for someone to devour. Resist him, standing firm in the faith..." (1 Peter 5:8-9 NIV) I know these verses can sound discouraging in a sense, but I'm asking you to look at the positives in them for a moment. The devil is constantly searching for someone to attack. That means he needs to actively look for believers who are vulnerable. If you and I will "resist him, standing firm in [our] faith," the enemy will have to pass us over, and go look for someone else to harass. How do we acquire this kind of strength against Satan's onslaught?

First, we must pray BEFORE temptation comes our way. Prayer helps to prepare us for satanic attack. It reminds the Lord – and us – that we cannot stand against temptation alone, and that we must lean heavily upon God for the victory. Jesus said: "Watch and pray so that you will not fall into temptation. The spirit is willing, but the body is weak." (Matthew 26:41

NIV) The Master is warning us to be ever watchful, and ever prayerful. We should purposely avoid people, places, and things that can tempt us in our areas of weakness. When that is not possible, we must pray ahead of time that the Lord will strengthen us, and help us to stand firm. We can use Jesus' own words – "Lead us not into temptation, but deliver us from the evil one." (Matthew 6:13 NIV) And we can pray God's own promises back to Him, trusting Him to keep His Word – "Lord, on the basis of Your Word, I am asking You to strengthen me, and to protect me from the evil one." (2 Thessalonians 3:3 NIV)

Second, we must rebuke the enemy with the Word of God, just as Jesus did when Satan came to tempt Him in the desert. (Luke 4:1-13) Each time the devil came against the Savior, He answered him with, "It is written," and then quoted Scripture. We have the privilege and responsibility to use the same tactic. That means, of course, that we must have a working knowledge of the Scriptures. We can ask the Lord to help us to study and memorize His Word, and He will do it. You may have trouble remembering where you put your car keys, but in the heat of battle, you will be able to declare Scripture after Scripture, if you plant it in your heart the way God tells us to. (Proverbs 4:20-22) As the Bible says, "God's Word is an indispensable weapon." (Ephesians 6:17 MSG)

Third, we must call on the Lord for help and deliverance, because as the apostle Peter wrote: "The Lord knows how to rescue the godly from temptation." (2 Peter 2:9 NASB) And He has a plan for our victory. Our flesh may tell us that we can't possibly resist the pressure the enemy is putting on us, but we must not buy into that lie. The truth is stated plainly in 1 Corinthians 10:13 (NASB): "No temptation has overtaken you but such as is common to man; and God is faithful, who will not allow you to be tempted beyond what you are able, but with the temptation will provide the way of escape also, that you may be able to endure it." This "way of escape" may be something as simple as casting down wrong thoughts, and replacing them with right ones. (2 Corinthians 10:3-5) We have to remember that temptation is a process, and we can interrupt that process with the help of God. Most importantly, we must continually remind ourselves of what Jesus went through on our behalf: "Because He himself suffered when He was tempted, He is able to help those who are being tempted." (Hebrews 2:18 NIV) You have awesome heavenly resources to help you win your battles with temptation through the power of God. Make the most of them – and receive the blessed victories He has in store for you!

Lord, I thank You that the devil can't throw anything at me that I can't handle with Your help. Teach me to avoid people, places, and things that are not Your best for me. Give me a growing passion for Your presence and Your Word, so that I may become strong in spirit. Thank You that in every situation and circumstance, You have a plan for my victory, and I will see it unfold as I follow Your lead!

Promise-Power Point: When I pray before I face temptation – when I use the Scriptures as a weapon and call on God for deliverance – He will equip me to overcome every temptation and trial for His glory.

Refusing a Fatalistic View

"That's why I urge you to pray for absolutely everything, ranging from small to large. Include everything as you embrace this God-life, and you'll get God's everything." Mark 11:24 MSG

I often hear from people whose jobs are at risk, or who have already lost their jobs, and they are some of the most heart-rending emails I receive. One man wrote me recently and said that his company was undergoing reorganization and restructuring, and many of its employees were being laid off. He explained how he desperately needed his job to support his family, and that because of his age and the job climate, it would be very difficult for him to find other employment. He asked me to pray that God would protect and preserve his position at his workplace, and he confessed that he was telling coworkers and loved ones that he expected his division to be completely eliminated within the next few months. I was stunned. On the one hand, this man wanted God to intervene to save his job, and on the other hand, he was predicting that his position would be eliminated in the near future. As I read over his email, it became clear to me that he had adopted a fatalistic view about his situation.

What is a fatalistic view? It's when someone believes that a certain outcome is determined in advance, and cannot be changed. A person who is a fatalist feels that whatever is "meant" to happen will indeed happen. Often, these people are expecting things to turn out badly, and they see no point in trying to change the outcome. In other words, these folks hear a negative report, and they are likely to believe that what the report predicts is inevitable. It could be something as minor as a weather report. Or it could be something as major as a serious health report from a doctor. Here's what's so wrong about this kind of attitude: it's totally unscriptural. In fact, it's satanic. Suppose you hear a rumor at your workplace that there is going to be a major layoff. The first thing the devil is going to do is to try to convince you that you are going to lose your job. He'll put people in your path that will say negative things about your position, your company, and the economy. He'll keep the negative reports coming until you truly believe that it is your destiny to lose your job. Then, either you won't pray at all, or you will pray prayers that have no real faith in them. And you will begin SPEAKING negatively about your company and your job situation to others. When you do that, you are getting out of agreement with God's plans for you, and into agreement with the devil's plans for you. And even if the Lord was prepared to preserve your job, you are likely to lose it because you have given Satan and his cohorts permission to rob you of God's best. Let's do a quick review of the difference between the devil and the Lord. Jesus said: "The thief comes only in order to steal and kill and destroy. I came that they may have and enjoy life, and have it in abundance (to the full, till it overflows)." (John 10:10 AMP) The "thief" is Satan, and if you let him, he will steal your job, your finances, your health, and your loved ones.

I meet a lot of Christians who believe that whatever happens in this world is basically God's will. That is simply not true. If it WERE true, Jesus would not have told us to pray to the Father, "May Your will be done on earth, as it is in heaven." (Matthew 6:10 NLT) And why would the Savior tell us over and over again things like, "Pray...Ask...Seek...Knock..." if our prayers would have no bearing on our outcome? I believe that some Christians are just spiritually lazy at times. It's easier for them to believe that nothing they do or say can have an effect on their lives and circumstances. If it did, they would have to monitor their thoughts, words, and actions very carefully. And for some Christians, that's too much work, and too great a responsibility. It's easier for them to sit back and just blame God for everything that happens, than to hold themselves accountable. Sadly, these people will never fulfill their God-given purpose or potential, and they can never enjoy the full blessing of the promises of God.

Jesus said, "It will be done just as you believed it would." (Matthew 8:13 NIV) I know this is a scary thought, but it's also a promising one, too. When we hear negative reports, we don't have to adopt a fatalistic response. We can pray in faith for the desires of our hearts, while asking for God's best in the situation, whatever that might be. Then we won't cooperate with the devil's plans for us by default. Are you ready to play a bigger role in your destiny according to God's will for you?

Lord, I don't want to be spiritually lazy. I want to receive every good thing that You have in store for me. Teach me how to cooperate with You to that end. Show me how to partner with You to receive the outcome You have for me in every situation and circumstance. Help me to pray in agreement with Your good plans and purposes for me. Guard me from speaking words of doubt and unbelief that will give the devil permission to rob me of the blessings, rewards, and opportunities that are my inheritance in Christ. Thank You that as I refuse to adopt a fatalistic mindset, I will experience and enjoy the abundant life You died to give me!

Promise-Powered Point: As a Christ-follower, God has gifted me with the ability and responsibility to have a certain amount of control over my outcomes, as I pray and obey Him in every matter that concerns me.

Better to Trust the Lord

"It is better to trust the Lord than to put confidence in people." Psalm 118:8 NLT

When my husband, Joe, began having severe pain in his neck, it got so bad that it gave him pounding headaches, and made his blood pressure rise alarmingly. When he went to see his doctor, a large growth was discovered in his neck. Two more doctors confirmed the presence of the growth through various medical tests. All of the doctors suspected cancer, and a specialist told Joe that his chances of having it were 90%. A biopsy was ordered, but could not be performed for at least three weeks. Joe and I both dreaded having to wait that long to get the proper diagnosis and treatment. My husband was suffering terribly, and it grieved me to see him in so much pain. Because of that, I made a decision. I decided that I was not going to wait on doctors to heal my husband. I was going to wait on God.

I began praying for Joe's healing like never before. I started tucking him in bed at night, and praying aloud over him, asking the Lord to heal him before his test date even arrived. I reminded God over and over that we were not waiting on doctors for Joe's healing, but we were waiting on Him. At one point, Joe told me, "One thing is for certain – I'm not getting out of this without surgery." He had heard the doctors' reports about the growth in his neck. Three different doctors had felt it, and it was confirmed by ultrasound tests. I knew I couldn't afford to have the same mindset that Joe had. God was challenging me to believe Him for greater things. And it was God's Word and promises that bolstered my faith. David wrote: "Some trust in chariots and some in horses, but we trust in the name of the Lord our God." (Psalm 20:7 NIV) The Holy Spirit brought this verse to my remembrance, and urged me not to put my confidence in doctors, but in God. The Lord could certainly use doctors as part of my husband's healing process, but I was not to put my faith in them, or to wait on them for help. As I prayed for Joe as though God was our only hope, we began to see some real improvements in his symptoms. The pain lessened. The swelling went down. Joe was no longer incapacitated, but was able to function normally. And we began to thank and praise God that His healing power was already at work in my husband's body.

Psalm 60:11-12 (NIV) says: "Give us aid against the enemy, for the help of man is worthless. With God we will gain the victory, and He will trample down our enemies." These words of David's kept coming to mind during this time, and I began praying them in faith whenever I was tempted to doubt. I confess there were times when I would hear the doctors' negative reports in my ears, and fear would start to rise in my heart. Then I would remind myself that Scripture instructs us to think only on "whatever things are of good report," and I would "cast down" those thoughts that did not agree with God's Word. (Philippians 4:8 NKJV; 2

Corinthians 10:5 KJV) A good doctor can be a godsend. And the Lord can, and often does, use doctors to heal us. But if we wait solely upon the medical profession for help, we could be waiting a very long time, often with very disappointing results to show for it. While the "help of man" can truly prove "worthless" at times, the help of God never will.

When the day finally came for Joe's biopsy, no growth could be found in his neck. The same type of medical tests that confirmed the growth's existence, confirmed its absence. And all final reports showed absolutely no cancer. The doctors can explain it any way they want to, but my family and I know that it was the hand of God that healed my husband, and we are giving Him all the glory. We have learned firsthand the truth of His Word – "It is better to trust the Lord than to put confidence in people." (Psalm 118:8 NLT)

Lord, forgive me for the times I misplaced my confidence, instead of keeping it in You. Give me a revelation of Your matchless power and love that will move me to trust in You alone from now on. Thank You that as I depend on You for all my needs, I will experience Your supernatural protection and provision!

Promise-Power Point: *When I seek God first in times of adversity, and keep my expectations in Him, He will show Himself strong on my behalf, and rescue me and mine.*

Our Dreams or His?

"If anyone intends to come after Me, let him deny himself [forget, ignore, disown, and lose sight of himself and his own interests]..." Mark 8:34 AMP

A young man wrote me recently and told me how he had begun sinking into a pit of depression, because a dream that he had as a young boy seemed to be dying. For years, he had been preparing for this dream to come to pass, and there were many times when it seemed like certain doors were being opened. Lately, though, doors had been closing, and he was now feeling defeated and alone. The bright future that he had set his hopes on was becoming hopelessly dim. As I read this young man's letter, I couldn't help realizing that somewhere along the line, he had gotten off track, and he had begun desperately seeking his dream, instead of God.

Unfortunately, this problem is all too common among Christians these days. Perhaps you have met some of these folks. They talk about THEIR dreams, THEIR visions, and THEIR desires. It's all about THEM. You rarely – if ever – hear them say things like: "I want to become the person God created me to be. I want to fulfill my God-given purpose and potential. I want to make a difference for God. I want to glorify God with the gifts He's given me." What these people don't realize – or want to realize – is that God has dreams, visions, and desires for them, too. And, in fact, His should take precedence over their own, because He is the One who created them for a specific purpose. As Scripture says: "We are God's [own] handiwork (His workmanship), recreated in Christ Jesus, [born anew] that we may do those good works which God predestined (planned beforehand) for us [taking paths which He prepared ahead of time], that we should walk in them [living the good life which He prearranged and made ready for us to live]." (Ephesians 2:10 AMP) Before we ever showed up on Planet Earth, God had specific plans and purposes mapped out for us, and it is up to us to discover what they are. We do that by walking in close fellowship with Him daily, seeking Him with an open and obedient heart. As we cooperate with the Lord, we see His awesome plans for us gradually unfold like a beautiful flower.

The Bible warns us against a sin called "selfish ambition". It's when we have a strong desire for achievement and success apart from God. Scripture says that selfish ambition is a "work of the flesh" (Galatians 5:19-20 NKJV), and that those who practice it "will not inherit the kingdom of God." (v. 21) Jesus said: "If any of you wants to be My follower, you must put aside your selfish ambition, shoulder your cross, and follow Me. If you try to keep your life for yourself, you will lose it. But if you give up your life for My sake and for the sake of the Good News, you will find true life." (Mark 8:33-35 NLT) I have seen Christians wear themselves out trying to make their dreams come to pass in their own strength. Many of them have extraordinary gifts and talents, but they live frustrated lives, because they refuse to surrender themselves and their futures to the Lord. They fail to realize that because they gave their lives to Christ at one point, God is committed to transforming them into the likeness of His Son. (Romans 8:29) Therefore, the Lord often opposes their proud and selfish attempts to glorify themselves, instead of Him. As Scripture says: "God sets Himself against the proud (the insolent, the overbearing, the disdainful, the presumptuous, the boastful) – [and He opposes, frustrates, and defeats them], but gives grace (favor, blessing) to the humble." (1 Peter 5:5 AMP) If they would only surrender their dreams and desires to the One who created them, they would experience His awesome plans for them, plans that would exceed their highest expectations in every way.

All of us will be asked to give up our dreams and visions sooner or later. This is a test of our devotion to the Lord, and it's a test that all of us must pass. If you can relate to this young man's situation today, I urge you to let your dreams go for now. Put them "on the altar," and begin focusing only upon your relationship with the Lord. As you learn to love, seek, and serve Him with all your heart, you will find that you won't have to pursue your dreams and desires, because they'll be pursuing YOU!

Lord, today I ask You to remove from me every dream and desire that is not from You. Plant Your plans and desires for my life firmly in my mind and heart, and bring them to pass according to Your perfect will and timing. When I am tempted to begin focusing on my dreams and desires too much, remind me that this kind of mindset could seriously delay my blessings. Thank You that as I wait upon You in faith and devotion, I will experience the divine destiny You have had in store for me all along!

Promise-Power Point: **When I get serious about seeking the Lord instead of seeking my dreams and desires, the fulfillment of my longings won't be delayed one moment longer than necessary.**

When Trouble Comes

"The Lord is good. When trouble comes, He is the place to go!" Nahum 1:7 TLB

The next time you face trouble of some sort, I want you to think about the kind of mindset you adopt in your situation. When trouble strikes, do you immediately think about Jesus' words in 16:33, "In this world you will have trouble"? Or does your mind promptly turn to one of the many promises of protection and deliverance in God's Word? I am going to do my best to help you to take a more positive stand against your troubles from now on, instead of a negative one. I believe that once you adopt a more hopeful outlook, you will be able to receive God's absolute best in your situation.

The first thing we need to do to remain positive in times of trouble is to turn to the Lord in prayer. Scripture says: "Is any one of you in trouble? He should pray." (James 5:13 NIV) When adversity strikes, do you run to the throne, or to the phone? Once we have failed to seek God first in a situation, we have already set ourselves up for defeat. The Lord may certainly direct us to others for advice or help at some point, but it is never His will for us to turn to others first. David, the shepherd-king, wrote: "In the day of my trouble I will call to You, for You will answer me." (Psalm 86:7 NIV) When trouble hit, David didn't despair, because he knew that he had options. He could call on the Most High God, with whom he had a personal relationship, and he could expect a divine, custom-made solution to his problem. You and I can have this same kind of assurance and hope. The Bible tells us that the Lord called David, "a man after My own heart". (Acts 13:22) I believe that one of the main reasons for this was that even though David had countless men, weapons, counselors, and other resources at his disposal, he didn't depend on them for help or deliverance. He wrote, "Give us help from trouble, for the help of man is useless." (Psalm 108:12 NKJV) If we rely on people or things for help, we won't be able to keep a positive perspective on our situation for very long, because sooner or later, they will bitterly disappoint us.

Another thing we need to do to face our troubles with a positive mindset is to claim and meditate on the promises of God. Psalm 91:7 (NIV) says: "A thousand may fall at your side, ten thousand at your right hand, but it will not come near you." In other words, we can be surrounded by trouble of the most serious kind, and we can claim supernatural protection and deliverance right in the midst of it. A later verse in this same psalm reveals that one reason this is possible is that the Lord assigns His angels to assist and protect us: "For He will give His angels [especial] charge over you to accompany and defend and preserve you in all your ways." (Psalm 91:11 AMP) Scripture reveals a connection between our prayers of distress and angelic activity: "In my desperation I prayed, and the Lord listened; He saved me from all my troubles. For the angel of the Lord is a guard; he surrounds and defends all who fear him." (Psalm 34:6-7 NLT) Doesn't it fill you with hope just to think of the Lord responding to your desperate pleas with the dispatching of His mighty angelic warriors? Some of the most inspiring promises in all of Scripture are contained in the fifteenth verse of Psalm 91 (NIV): "He will call upon Me, and I will answer him; I will be with him in trouble, I will deliver him and honor him." When I claim these supernatural promises in times of trouble, I am declaring that: (1) I can expect the Lord to answer my prayers for help; (2) I will not be alone, but I will have the presence of Almighty God; (3) I will witness the delivering power of the Lord on my behalf; and (4) I will be better than ever, having experienced my trials.

Yes, it's true that Jesus told us, "In this world you will have trouble." But that's not the end of the story. He went on to say, "But take heart! I have overcome the world." (John 16:33 NIV) In other words, even though we will face difficult times before we get to heaven, we should be encouraged by the fact that our union with Christ will enable us to overcome whatever comes our way. The Lord has given us the privilege of prayer, and the power of His promises, along with a host of other resources, to help us face our troubles with hope in our hearts. Let's make the most of these heavenly resources, so that we may be a beacon of hope to others, and become all God created us to be!

Lord, whenever trouble comes my way, help me to resist becoming negative, angry, or depressed. Enable me to see my situation from Your perspective, and to believe in Your ability and willingness to protect and deliver me and mine. Thank You that as I turn to You first in prayer, and claim Your promises of victory, I will triumph over my troubles every time!

Promise-Power Point: Because God is good, He will show Himself strong on my behalf in difficult times when I pray in faith for His assistance, and stand on His promises of deliverance and victory.

Strongholds of Human Reasoning

"We are human, but we don't wage war as humans do. We use God's mighty weapons, not worldly weapons, to knock down the strongholds of human reasoning and to destroy false arguments. We destroy every proud obstacle that keeps people from knowing God. We capture their rebellious thoughts and teach them to obey Christ." 2 Corinthians 10:3-4 NLT

When I heard that a Hollywood studio was in the process of making a new motion picture about Moses and the Israelites' exodus from Egypt, I already knew that some people would ask for my opinion on the Bible account of this event. I've heard it all before. "Do you really believe that the Red Sea was parted the way the Bible says it was? It's simply impossible!" I have gotten used to the funny looks on people's faces when I tell them that I believe that every word of it is true.

This wasn't always the case, however. I was quite the skeptic myself until about 22 years ago, when I surrendered my life to Christ for real, and I told the Lord that from then on, by His grace, I would take Him at His Word. I had heard the testimony of one of the greatest evangelists of our time, who said that his life radically changed when He made a quality decision to believe that the Bible was true. He confessed to the Lord that he didn't understand how remarkable biblical accounts, such as the story of Jonah, could be genuine, but he was determined to shake off his doubts, and to live his life as though God was true to His Word. Since then, this man has brought literally millions of people to Christ.

Jesus said, "Truly I say to you, unless you are converted and become like children, you will not enter the kingdom of heaven." (Matthew 18:3 NASB) Adopting the faith of a child is part of our conversion experience! What is the attitude of a child that the Savior is referring to here? It's an attitude of trust. It's the same attitude that Abraham had when God told him that he was going to be the father of many nations, even though he and his wife were still childless in their old age. Scripture tells us: "[Abraham] did not weaken in faith when he considered the [utter] impotence of his own body, which was as good as dead because he was about a hundred years old, or [when he considered] the barrenness of Sarah's [deadened] womb. No unbelief or distrust made him waver (doubtingly question) concerning the promise of God, but he grew strong and was empowered by faith as he gave praise and glory to God, fully satisfied and assured that God was able and mighty to keep His word and to do what He had promised." (Romans 4:19-21 AMP) Abraham was commended and blessed by the Lord because he didn't "doubtingly question" God's promise to him. It amazes me how many Christians doubtingly question the veracity of the Scriptures. It's no wonder, then, that they never reap the full benefits of God's "precious and magnificent promises," even though these 7,000 promises are their inheritance in Christ. (2 Peter 1:4 NASB)

When the apostle Paul teaches us about spiritual warfare in the Scriptures, he writes: "We are human, but we don't wage war as humans do. We use God's mighty weapons, not worldly weapons, to knock down the strongholds of human reasoning and to destroy false arguments. We destroy every proud obstacle that keeps people from knowing God. We capture their rebellious thoughts and teach them to obey Christ." (2 Corinthians 10:3-4 NLT) Notice the phrase, "strongholds of human reasoning". This means that Satan comes against us with thoughts, mindsets, and attitudes which are contrary to the Word of God, which are all designed to keep us from knowing the truth about God. These "rebellious thoughts" might not keep us from being saved, but they will likely keep us from receiving the good things that God has promised Christ followers in His Word – including gifts of protection, provision, and healing.

In Galatians, Paul says: "Dear brothers and sisters, I want you to understand that the gospel message I preach is not based on mere human reasoning. I received my message from no human source, and no one taught me. Instead, I received it by direct revelation from Jesus Christ." (Galatians 1:10-12 NLT) No matter how hard we try, we cannot "reason" someone into the kingdom of God. They can only receive the Gospel message as truth through revelation from the Holy Spirit. That's because, as Paul says, the Good News is "not based on mere human reasoning". It makes absolutely no sense to the human mind apart from God. As Paul says elsewhere in the Scriptures: "The message of the cross is foolish to those who are headed for destruction! But we who are being saved know it is the very power of God." (1 Corinthians 1:18 NLT)

So you and I have a choice as Christians. We can decide to live and act as though the Bible were true, and we can receive the full benefits of the divine promises it contains. Or, we can allow doubt, disguised as human reasoning, to rob us of the good things that are our rightful inheritance in Christ. Jesus says to us every day in every instance, "Did I not tell you that if you believe, you will see the glory of God?" (John 11:40 NIV) Are you prepared to put aside your doubts, and to see more of God's glory manifested in your life and circumstances than you ever have before?

Lord, You once told Your disciple Thomas, "Stop doubting and believe!" (John 20:27 NIV) I pray that for myself this day, and I ask that You help me to cooperate with You for the building of my faith. Help me to spend time each day being still in Your presence – praying, reading Your Word, and listening for Your voice. Remind me that it's Your Word that renews my mind and makes me resistant to the kind of human reasoning that robs me of Your best. Thank You that as I choose to believe Your truth, no person on earth, and no devil in hell will be able to keep me from reaping the full benefits of Your magnificent promises!

Promise-Power Point: When I make a quality decision to "stop doubting and believe" the Word of God in its entirety, I will open the door to see God's glory manifested in my life, my family, my ministry, and in every one of my circumstances.

I Desire to Do Your Will

"I desire to do Your will, O my God." Psalm 40:8 NIV

When I had a major decision to make not long ago, and I sought the Lord about it, He reminded me of a passage in Scripture that describes David's course of action in a serious situation. David and his army had been away, when a band of Amalekites raided their homes and set them on fire. All of the women and children were taken captive and carried off. (See 1 Samuel 30:1-2) At this horrifying discovery, "David and his men wept aloud until they had no strength left to weep." (v. 4) But David's troubles didn't stop there. The Bible goes on to say: "David was greatly distressed because the men were talking of stoning him; each one was bitter in spirit because of his sons and daughters." (v. 6) How David responds to this series of disturbing events is what the Lord wanted me to focus on. Scripture says: "And David inquired of the Lord, 'Shall I pursue this raiding party? Will I overtake them?'" God's response to His faithful servant is: "Pursue them... You will certainly overtake them and succeed in the rescue." (v. 8) The result? "David recovered everything the Amalekites had taken... Nothing was missing." (1 Samuel 30:18,19 NIV)

The first thing I took note of in this passage was that David's situation was serious, and it demanded immediate attention, especially since people's lives were at stake. Yet David still paused long enough to seek the Lord's wisdom and guidance. The second thing that impressed me was that David must have had strong desires of his own in the matter. His own loved ones were in peril, and there's no doubt that he desperately wanted to jump on his horse and go after them without delay. Yet he didn't allow his emotions to sweep him away and cause him to do something rash. He put his own feelings on hold while he "inquired of the Lord."

The fact that David was fully equipped to act on his own, but didn't, may have struck me the most. Here was a man who many scholars consider the most fearsome and accomplished warrior of all time hesitating to rise to action when his own loved ones were at risk. God Himself called David "a man of war" who had "shed much blood." (1 Chronicles 28:3) Yet his determination to seek the Lord before he took action shows why God also called him "a man after My own heart." (Acts 13:22 NIV)

Finally, David did not allow threats from his own men to manipulate him into making a hasty decision that he might regret in the end. Instead, he focused on what the Lord would have him do in the situation, and he resolved to follow His God.

At the end of this passage, David declares: "[The Lord] has protected us and handed over to us the forces that came against us." (1 Samuel 30:23 NIV) Because David consulted the Lord and followed His lead, God protected him and his loved ones, and enabled him to defeat his enemies. When you and I follow David's example, we will have all the help of Heaven on our side, and we will gain the victory in Christ!

Lord, teach me how to live a surrendered life before You. Guard me from all willfulness, stubbornness, and pride. Give me a heart like David's when he declared, "I desire to do Your will, O my God." (Psalm 40:8) Thank You that as I determine to seek You and Your guidance and direction – and do my best to obey You – I will experience life at its very best!

Promise-Powered Point: When I have a decision to make, if I refuse to act hastily, and instead seek the Lord's will for my life, I will experience the best possible outcome as I follow His lead all the way.

Revenge is Sweet!

"Those who are kind benefit themselves, but the cruel bring ruin on themselves." Proverbs 11:17 NIV

Years ago, when my sons were very young, my family and I used to watch a lot of baseball on TV. In many of those games, we witnessed pitchers deliberately hitting players on the opposite team with the ball. Sometimes, the unlucky victim was quick to retaliate with harsh words or punches. Other times, the player who was struck was calm and composed, and continued to do his best at the plate. No doubt, it was this player's goal to follow his coach's wise advice to exact the best revenge by hitting a home run off the offending pitcher, and beating the other team. This whole scenario came to mind recently when I was listening to a godly man preaching about forgiveness, and he said that when someone hurts us, forgiveness is ultimately the best revenge, because it liberates and empowers us to move into all God has for us. This man's words really spoke to my heart, and I made a quality decision that day that I was no longer going to let anyone or anything prevent me from receiving all the good things that the Lord had in store for me.

The Bible has a lot to say about the subject of forgiveness. One reason for that is because refusing to forgive others drives a wedge between us and God. It hinders our closeness and communication with Him.

And it causes division between us and others, poisoning our relationships. Scripture says: "Let every man be quick to hear [a ready listener], slow to speak, slow to take offense and to get angry." (James 1:19 AMP) This verse contains some of the best advice we could ever apply to our relationships, but the part that I have had to remind myself of most is to be "slow to take offense". It seems as though in recent years, our society has tried to make becoming offended a virtue, and an honorable means of getting our needs met. But that's not God's way. His Word tells us: "A man's wisdom gives him patience; it is to his glory to overlook an offense." (Proverbs 19:11 NIV) Sometimes, in order for us to get the upper hand in a situation, all we have to do is refuse to get offended, and God will do the rest.

It has been rightly said that bitterness is like taking poison, hoping that your enemy will die. How stupid is that? And yet many of us do this very thing, by refusing to forgive someone after they hurt us. My husband, Joe, and I have been together for more than 40 years. You can't have an intimate relationship with someone for that long without hurting and offending each other at times. I decided a long time ago that when Joe and I have disagreements or arguments of any kind, I am going to forgive him quickly and thoroughly, so that I don't do myself harm. Perhaps that sounds selfish to you, but to me, it's simply the smart thing to do. And you know what? It's scriptural, too.

Scripture says: "If your enemy is hungry, give him food to eat; if he is thirsty, give him water to drink. In doing this, you will heap burning coals on his head, and the Lord will reward you." (Proverbs 25:21-22 NIV) Here is a formula for getting the best kind of revenge when someone has hurt us. Instead of retaliating, we demonstrate the love of Christ, putting ourselves in a position to receive extraordinary blessings and rewards from God that we can't have any other way. The Bible reassures us that it pays to be kind: "The merciful, kind, and generous man benefits himself [for his deeds return to bless him]." (Proverbs 11:17 AMP) But look what it says will happen to troublemakers: "They make trouble, but it backfires on them. They plan violence for others, but it falls on their own heads." (Psalm 7:16 NLT) Let's face it, it is just plain smart to treat people right, even when we are not being treated right ourselves.

If each time someone upsets or wounds us, we ask the Lord how He would have us respond, we will usually sense Him telling us to pray for these people, and maybe even to extend an act of kindness that might get their attention and draw them to Him. Whatever it is, if we will do it with a good attitude, drawing on the supernatural power that abides in us through the Holy Spirit, we will be richly rewarded. And most importantly, the Lord will be glorified. My heartfelt prayer for you is that you will put these principles to work the next time you are feeling hurt or offended, so that you may discover for yourself that *revenge is sweet!*

Lord, when I am tempted to harbor resentment or unforgiveness toward someone, remind me that my disobedience will shut off Your work in my life, and cause me to become stuck and stagnant. Remind me that my decision to forgive doesn't make them right, but it makes me free. I praise You, Lord, that the way of forgiveness is the path to progress, promotion, and peace!

Promise-Power Point: I am not doomed to live in bondage to bitterness, resentment, or unforgiveness – but I am equipped to walk in supernatural freedom and victory as I walk in obedience to Christ.

Praying for "Snakes"

"Which of you, if his son asks for bread, will give him a stone? Or if he asks for a fish, will give him a snake? If you, then, though you are evil, know how to give good gifts to your children, how much more will your Father in heaven give good gifts to those who ask Him!"
Matthew 7:9-11 NIV

A while back, I received a letter from a young woman who felt desperate and needed prayer. A certain young man had caught her attention by repeatedly flirting with her. She, in turn, did everything she could to try to win his heart, and yet she eventually discovered that his true love was someone else entirely. Exasperated, she began earnestly praying that the Lord would make a way for her to be with her dream man. When her prayers went unanswered, she turned to me for advice. Her fervent plea nearly broke my heart – "Please pray for me in this situation, and if you have any idea why the Lord would be keeping him from loving me, then please write and let me know what you think!" After I sought the Lord about how I should respond to this woman, I shared with her Jesus' words in Matthew 7:9-11 (NLT): "You parents – if your children ask for a loaf of bread, do you give them a stone instead? Or if they ask for a fish, do you give them a snake? Of course not! If you sinful people know how to give good gifts to your children, how much more will your heavenly

Father give good gifts to those who ask Him." I told her that even though she might not want to hear the truth, it was very likely that the Lord was keeping this young man from her because he was a "snake" to her. I told her that she had two choices: She could insist on having her own way – and get involved in a relationship that was not God's best for her, risking a lifetime of regret – or she could put her trust in the Lord, and humbly and patiently wait upon Him for the blessed relationship He had planned for her.

I know from personal experience what it's like to be involved with a "snake". Before I met my husband, I wasted three years of my life in a relationship that was out of God's will for me. For a long time afterwards, I carried around a multitude of emotional scars from this negative experience, and I discovered firsthand how being in a wrong relationship can have devastating effects on every area of a person's life. The Bible says: "Above all else, guard your affections. For they influence everything else in your life." (Proverbs 4:23 TLB) Thankfully, the Lord sent me my husband, Joe, and He helped me to put enough of my past hurts behind me to embrace this relationship as His best for me. We have been happily married for almost 40 years now, and I have never regretted choosing God's will.

Just before Jesus talks about the good gifts that God wants to give us, He says: "Ask and it will be given to you; seek and you will find; knock and the door will be opened to you. For everyone who asks receives; he who seeks finds; and to him who knocks, the door will be opened." (Matthew 7:7-8 NIV) The Savior urges us to earnestly pray for our needs and desires, but He reminds us that we would be wise to trust God with the answers. I have raised two sons, and I can tell you that when my children have asked me for something that I know would do them more harm than good, as a loving parent, I would not give it to them. If we truly believe that God loves us and wants what is best for us, we will learn to put our wholehearted trust in Him when He chooses not to answer our prayers the way we had hoped.

Just as God wants us to desire and receive good things from Him, Satan wants us to desire and receive evil things from himself. (John 10:10) He will tempt us with wrong relationships and wrong opportunities of every kind. He will do everything he can to keep us from trusting God, and from waiting upon Him for His best. But we can choose God's will in every situation and circumstance, if we will follow the leading of the Holy Spirit who dwells in us. What "snakes" are you praying for today? Ask the Lord to reveal them to you, and to help you lay hold of the "good gifts" He has in store for you!

Lord, thank You for inviting me to "ask, seek, and knock". When I desire or pray for "snakes," I ask that You reveal it to me, and change my heart so that I can receive Your very best. Don't let me waste a single moment wanting or praying for things that are out of Your will. Today, I choose to believe and cling to Your precious promise which says – "Every good and perfect gift is from above"! (James 1:17 NIV)

Promise-Power Point: Only God knows for sure who and what are best for me, and as I put my trust in Him, and wait on Him for His perfect will, I will receive the relationships and plans that He has ordained for me.

Superabundantly!

"Now to Him Who, by (in consequence of) the [action of His] power that is at work within us, is able to [carry out His purpose and] do superabundantly, far over and above all that we [dare] ask or think [infinitely beyond our highest prayers, desires, thoughts, hopes, or dreams] – to Him be glory..." Ephesians 3:20-21 AMP

For the first 17 years that my husband, Joe, and I lived in our current home in Eastern Pennsylvania, he had to travel out-of-state to make a decent wage. Some jobs had him commuting up to 150 miles a day, so I prayed for years that the Lord would provide him with a good-paying job closer to home. One day, I felt impressed to "stretch" my faith and my prayers, and I began to pray, "Lord, do superabundantly above all we ask or imagine in Joe's job situation now." Suddenly, God opened a door for my husband to acquire a desirable position at a local company – not just any company, but the one that offers the highest paying jobs in our region of Pennsylvania. To top it off, Joe's new employer gave him an even higher starting salary than he had asked for.

I confess to being guilty of praying "just" or "only" prayers in the past. "Lord, if You will 'just' do this, I'll be happy." Or, "Lord, if You will 'only' do this, I won't ask You for another thing." It finally dawned on me one day that prayers like these do absolutely nothing for my faith. They don't challenge me, and they don't encourage my spiritual growth, or my intimacy with God. And they rarely result in spectacular answers from heaven. Scripture says that God is able to do "superabundantly, far over and above all that we [dare] ask or think [infinitely beyond our highest prayers, desires, thoughts, hopes, or dreams]." (Ephesians 3:20 AMP) While God is "able" to exceed our highest expectations in our lives and circumstances, He requires our cooperation in the process. These kinds of blessings are not automatic. If they were, we would see more of God's children walking in superabundant blessings. In order to do our part, we have to "ask". In other words, we have to pray. Too often, we hear believers say things like, "The Lord knows what I want. I don't need to ask Him for that." Yes, it's true that He knows everything before we tell Him about it, but asking demonstrates our humble dependence upon Him, and our belief that He hears us when we pray. Look through the Gospels and notice how many times Jesus instructs us to "ask". And don't miss the fact that He always attaches blessings to the act of asking.

Another thing we must do to receive superabundant blessings from God is to "think," or "imagine," as some translations say. Take a moment and think about a need or desire you have right now. Begin to imagine what you would like to see happening in this matter. Don't just think about an ordinary outcome, but imagine the biggest and best result you possibly can. Then ask the Lord to exceed your highest expectations. Do you want God to do something new and wonderful in your job situation, or in your finances? Is there a relationship that you want Him to bless you with, or to improve? Do you want the Lord to enable you to excel as a student, employee, or minister of the Gospel? Do you want Him to bless you with more creativity and skill? How about Him enabling you to finally overcome that sin that has been plaguing you for so long? Don't wait until you feel deserving to pray "superabundant" prayers. If you do, you will never pray them. Instead, go ahead and pray them in faith, trusting that the Lord will show you whatever it is you need to do to partner with Him to bring His highest blessings and purposes to pass in your life.

Notice how the Scripture uses the word "dare". The Lord is issuing us a challenge today. Will we dare to ask and believe Him for greater things than ever before?

Lord, I regret the times that I prayed "anemic" prayers, or no prayers at all. Give me the faith I need to believe You for all of the great things that You long to do in, for, and through me. Fill me with a growing passion for Your presence and Your Word, so that I can partner with You for the building of my faith. Thank You that my "superabundant" prayers will reap a harvest of blessings that will enrich my life and bring You glory!

Promise-Power Point: When I throw aside my indifference and my doubts, and begin to pray with a firm confidence in God and His promises, He will provide me with superabundant answers to my prayers.

Our True Standard

"For those God foreknew He also predestined to be conformed to the likeness of His Son." Romans 8:29 NIV

I recently heard from a young man who writes me occasionally for prayer and encouragement. He was going through some severe trials, and as he began to express his growing discouragement and frustration, he said things like – "I'm a good person. I'm better than most people. I don't do half the things that other people do." When I told him that his focus was wrong, and that instead of comparing himself to others, he should compare himself to Christ, he was stunned. Suddenly, his subtle "God owes me" attitude evaporated, and his sense of pride gave way to humility.

The Bible makes it clear that the Christian's standard should be Christ Himself, and that God's priority is for His children to be conformed to the image of His Son. Romans 8:29 (NIV) says, "For those God foreknew He also predestined to be conformed to the likeness of His Son." Scripture also tells us that believers "are being transformed into His likeness with ever-increasing glory, which comes from the Lord, who is the Spirit." (2 Corinthians 3:18 NIV) Our degree of cooperation with the Holy Spirit will help determine the speed and extent of this transformation. The more sensitive and obedient we are to the Spirit's leading on a day-to-day basis, the more spiritual progress we will make, and the more we will accomplish for the kingdom of God. We will never attain perfection in this life, but perfection should be our goal. The apostle Paul wrote, "Aim for perfection". (2 Corinthians 13:11 NIV) Although a spiritual giant, Paul freely admitted that he had a long way to go to become like Christ. However, that didn't stop him from pressing on. In Philippians 3:12 (MSG) he says: "I don't mean to say that I have already achieved these things or that I have already reached perfection! But I keep working toward that day when I will finally be all that Christ Jesus saved me for and wants me to be." While God does not expect us to model perfection, He does expect us to model growth.

In his second letter to the Corinthians, Paul condemns those who were setting their own standards of measurement, instead of using God's. He says: "Not that we [have the audacity to] venture to class or [even to] compare ourselves with some who exalt and furnish testimonials for themselves! However, when they measure themselves with themselves and compare themselves with one another, they are without understanding and behave unwisely." (2 Corinthians 10:12 AMP) When we measure ourselves against ourselves, or against others, we may become puffed up with pride because we think we are superior somehow. But measuring ourselves by God's standards can be wonderfully pride-deflating, which can lead to our treating people better, and our having a teachable spirit before the Lord. Paul goes on to say: "For [it is] not [the man] who praises and commends himself who is approved and accepted, but [it is the person] whom the Lord accredits and commends." (2 Corinthians 10:18 AMP) We should always be focused on seeking God's approval, rather than the approval of others, or even ourselves. This will protect us from becoming self-satisfied and self-righteous, as well as from becoming people-pleasers.

Some statements that we should watch out for in our speech are: "I'm not as bad as..." or "I'm better than..." or "At least I don't... or "I would never..." Statements like these could indicate that we are measuring ourselves against others, instead of Christ. We would be wise to monitor our thoughts in this area, too. Do we ever think to ourselves — "I'm a better parent, grandparent, son, daughter, sister, brother, worker, employee, manager, boss, neighbor, Christian, minister, preacher, writer, musician, artist..."? These are thoughts saturated with pride, and they are offensive to God. Do you want to fulfill your God-given purpose and potential in this life? Then you must make it your goal to "become more and more like [Christ]" all the time. (2 Corinthians 3:18 NLT) Make Jesus your standard, and lay hold of the life of victory, abundance, and purpose that He has in store for you!

Lord, please forgive me for the times I elevated myself at the expense of others in thought, word, or deed. When I am tempted to be arrogant or self-righteous, remind me that Christ is to be my true standard, and that next to Him, I have no basis for pride. Thank You that as I set my sights on becoming more like Jesus, I will reap the heavenly and earthly rewards of a Christ-centered life!

Promise-Power Point: If I will live as though Christ is my one true standard, He will bless me and use me in new and exciting ways for His glory.

Benefits and Blessings from God

"The merciful, kind, and generous man benefits himself [for his deeds return to bless him], but he who is cruel and callous [to the wants of others] brings on himself retribution." Proverbs 11:17 AMP

Last winter brought more ice and snow to the East Coast than my husband, Joe, and I had ever seen in our 60+ years. The worst part was that as soon as one storm was over, another one was on its way. Joe would be out there morning and night using his snow blower on our property, and then using it to help neighbors who had no snow blower of their own. It was hard work, especially for someone like Joe who had suffered a heart attack one year, and then undergone open-heart surgery another. Nevertheless, Joe wasn't the type to turn his back on a neighbor in need, so storm after storm, he labored to clear away the snow and ice for us, and for others.

All those storms were very hard on our old snow blower, and one day, our old machine refused to start. So Joe began the hard task of shoveling our long driveway and walkways by hand. I was busy inside our house, and when it dawned on me that I hadn't heard the familiar sound of our snow blower, I took a peek outside one of our front windows. What I saw made tears spring to my eyes. Two of our neighbors who didn't have snow blowers were busy shoveling our driveway, while Joe stood by trying to catch his breath. One of these neighbors was an elderly gentleman who never shoveled his own property, but always hired someone younger and more able to do it. The other neighbor was the man who hired himself out to our elderly neighbor, to earn some extra money to pay his bills. Both were neighbors that Joe had helped out many times when storms had covered their property with ice and snow.

As I watched this scene of neighborly love, I thought about Solomon's words in the Book of Proverbs: "The merciful, kind, and generous man benefits himself [for his deeds return to bless him]." (Proverbs 11:17 AMP) Another proverb of the wise king in this chapter says: "A generous man will prosper; he who refreshes others will himself be refreshed." (Proverbs 11:25 NIV) You see, our God is a generous God, and He calls His people to follow His example. He does this, not just so we can be a blessing to others, but so we will benefit ourselves. The apostle Paul put it this way: "[Remember] this: he who sows sparingly and grudgingly will also reap sparingly and grudgingly, and he who sows generously [that blessings may come to someone] will also reap generously and with blessings." (2 Corinthians 9:6 AMP) Even if we don't receive rewards for our acts of generosity from other people, God will reward us Himself. I know this from experience because when I have labored long and hard without any apparent reward for my efforts, the Lord has led me to claim His promise in Isaiah 49:4 (NIV): "But I said, 'I have labored in vain; I have spent my strength for nothing at all. Yet what is due me is in the Lord's hand, and my reward is with my God.'" And I have witnessed God sending me blessings that I never could have imagined, or even asked for. The Bible says, "Kindness makes a man attractive." (Proverbs 19:22 TLB) Are you ready to get better looking God's way?

Lord, forgive me for the times that You've sent opportunities my way to be a blessing to others, and I didn't make the most of them. Give me a generous and compassionate heart like Yours, so that I will be eager to reach out to others using the strength and the skills You've blessed me with. Help me to have pure motives that are pleasing to You when I lend someone a hand. Thank You that when my efforts are unappreciated and overlooked, my benefits and rewards will come from You!

Promise-Power Point: God has rewards and bonuses for me that I can only receive when I use my time, talents, and treasure to bless someone else.

Don't Measure Short

"Then He said to them, 'Take heed what you hear. With the same measure you use, it will be measured to you; and to you who hear, more will be given.'" Mark 4:24 NKJV

Earlier this year, the Lord began dealing with me about how I was failing to reap the full benefit of His Word and promises. He started with a verse from Deuteronomy 7:15 (NIV), which says, "The Lord will keep you free from every disease." This particular Scripture was very familiar to me. For years, I had prayed it over my family, and had claimed it as my own. God made me realize that I was measuring this promise short by not truly believing that He would keep my loved ones and me free from EVERY disease. I had repeatedly spoken this Scripture with my lips, but I did not believe in my heart that the Lord really meant "every" disease. To my own natural mind, it seemed unreasonable that in a fallen world, I could ask or expect God to keep His Word in this case. But once I sensed the Lord's challenge, I decided to take a leap of faith and to start praying and expecting the total deliverance this verse promises.

As if to remind me of His challenge, the Lord led me to some passages in Scripture the other day which record some of Jesus' teachings on sowing the Word of God. In Mark 4:20 (NKJV), He says: "But these are the ones sown on good ground, those who hear the word, accept it, and bear fruit: some thirtyfold, some sixty, and some a hundred." Notice that those who receive the Word in a good heart will not all bear the same amount of fruit; some will bear more than others. In the same passage, the Savior reveals why. "Take heed what you hear. With the same measure you use, it will be measured to you; and to you who hear, more will be given." (Mark 4:24 NKJV) The NASB translation says, "By your standard of measure it will be measured to you." In other words, how we hear and measure the Word of God will determine the measure of fruit we will reap from it. When you hear or read that the Lord has promised to supply ALL your needs (Philippians 4:19), do you really hear "all," or do you make excuses based on doubt or reasoning? Remember, Jesus said that "to you who hear, MORE will be given." Do you want to be included in the "more" category? Then you are going to have to stop measuring God's promises short.

In the following verse in Mark 4, Jesus says: "For whoever has, to him more will be given; but whoever does not have, even what he has will be taken away from him." (Mark 4:26 NKJV) We find out earlier in this passage that God is not the one who robs us of the Word or its fruit, but the enemy. Mark 4:15 (NIV) says: "As soon as they hear it, Satan comes and takes away the word that was sown in them." One way that we allow Satan to steal the Word from us is to refuse to believe that God means EXACTLY what He says. When Scripture says that the Lord delivers us from ALL our fears (Psalm 34:4), do you really believe that you can live totally free from fear, or do you reserve the right to hang on to some of them?

When we measure God's Word short, we put limits on His work in our lives, and in the lives of others. But when we get into agreement with the Word, we reap untold amounts of fruit – for our good and His glory. The Lord is challenging you and me today to prove our belief in the power and truth of His Word by applying it to our specific situations and petitions. When we do, He will move heaven and earth to honor His promises to us!

Lord, forgive me for all of the times I measured Your Word short, and failed to reap the abundant harvest You had for me. Give me a believing heart, and teach me how to take You at Your Word from now on. Thank You that as I believe that You mean exactly what You say, You will bless me and use me in extraordinary ways for Your glory!

Promise-Power Point: When I truly believe that God's Word is true, and that He is true to His Word, He will honor and reward my faith in unusual and extraordinary ways.

Experiencing God

"Those who obey My commandments are the ones who love Me. And because they love Me, My Father will love them, and I will love them. And I will reveal Myself to each one of them." John 14:21 NLT

The other day, I received a heartbreaking letter from a woman who writes me occasionally for prayer and encouragement. She longed to have an intimate relationship with God, but she felt that whenever she prayed and tried to talk to Him, all she got was silence. She admitted that she was not living a godly lifestyle, but she was convinced that years of unanswered prayers had a lot to do with her lack of devotion. She said that the nature of God that was revealed in the Scriptures did not match up with what she was seeing in her own life. How was she supposed to know God's will for her life, and follow His direction, if she couldn't even hear His voice?

I explained to this lady that even though God loves each and every one of us, not all of us will experience that love. Only those who humble themselves before the Lord with a truly repentant heart can have an intimate relationship with Him. Receiving Christ as our Savior is a part of this process, but we must go further than that. We must make Jesus the LORD of every area of our lives. That means that we must walk in humble obedience to His will for us on a day-to-day basis.

Look at this verse: "The person who has My commands and keeps them is the one who [really] loves Me; and whoever [really] loves Me will be loved by My Father, and I [too] will love him and will show (reveal, manifest) Myself to him. [I will let Myself be clearly seen by him and make Myself real to him.]" (John 14:21 AMP) Here, Jesus promises that He and the Father will not only love us, but that they will REVEAL themselves to us, when we set our minds and hearts on obeying the commands of God. We cannot expect to experience the good plans that the Lord has in store for us if we refuse to obey His Word, or to follow the leadership of His Spirit. Jesus said, "My sheep hear My voice and I know them, and they follow Me." (John 10:27 NKJV) This usually doesn't mean that we will hear an audible voice when the Lord speaks to us, but that we will sense little "impressions" in our spirit that will point us in a certain direction. If you are having serious trouble hearing from God on a regular basis, either you have not truly surrendered your life to Him and experienced the new birth, or you are not spending enough time in His presence and His Word. Psalm 119:105 (NLT) says: "Your Word is a lamp for my feet and a light for my path." If we don't have a working knowledge of the Scriptures, there will be times when it will be nearly impossible for us to discern the will of God.

I told this woman that even though it was God's heartfelt desire to bless her more than she could ever imagine, He wasn't about to do that when she was living an ungodly lifestyle, or compromising her Christian walk. The Bible says, "Your sins keep My blessings at a distance." (Jeremiah 5:25 MSG) For most of my life, I was a Christian who felt like God was always at a distance. When I finally surrendered my life to the Lord, and got serious about studying and obeying His Word, I began experiencing the presence, the power, and the goodness of God on a daily basis. I had to make a lot of sacrifices, and so will you. Is it difficult? Yes. Is it worth it? YES! The Lord wants us to get ready answers to our prayers. But He expects us to do our part. Jesus said, "If you live in Me [abide vitally united to Me] and My words remain in you and continue to live in your hearts, ask whatever you will, and it shall be done for you." (John 15:7 AMP) Even if you have prayed a salvation prayer before, I encourage you to pray the one below with all your heart, and open the door for God to do a new and mighty work in you – and in your relationship with Him – as you surrender your life to Him anew!

Heavenly Father, please forgive me for my sins. I believe that Jesus died on the cross for my sins, and I receive Him today as my personal Savior and Lord. I surrender to You all that I am, and all that I have, holding nothing back. Make me the person You created me to be, and equip me to fulfill my God-given purpose and potential. Teach me how to live the supernatural, abundant, resurrection life that Jesus died for me to have. Thank You for filling me with Your Spirit, and making me a Christ-follower and a world-changer for Your glory!

***Promise-Power Point:** When I make a quality decision to live a surrendered life before the Lord, I will experience His awesome presence and power in every area of my life, and in every circumstance that I submit to Him.*

Do the Right Thing

Never tire of doing what is right." 2 Thessalonians 3:13 NIV

When my husband's company decided to move across the country years ago, Joe and I decided not to move with them. Many employees were bitter about the move. Some felt obligated to go with the company, and were resentful about being separated from family and friends. Others felt that moving was not an option for them, and were indignant about being left behind. My husband had a totally different attitude. Even though he elected not to move with his company, he cheerfully and wholeheartedly got busy helping with the move. As soon as he did, some of his coworkers began questioning him. "Why are you helping with this move? You're being left behind!" Some even eyed him suspiciously, asking, "What's in it for you?" Joe would just smile and say that he was doing it simply because he believed it was the right thing to do.

Years ago, I heard a godly man say: "Do the right thing. Do it because it's right. Do it right." I have thought about this man's message many times over the years, and I have even posted his words of wisdom on my kitchen refrigerator for everyone to see. No doubt, my husband's attitude toward his company's move was influenced by these powerful principles. As Joe made up his mind to do what he thought was the right thing in a difficult situation, he became downright joyful. And this is actually scriptural because the Bible says, "You're one happy man when you do what's right, one happy woman when you form the habit of justice." (Psalm 106:3 MSG) While my husband was surrounded by sour faces, he was able to wear a smile. Don't you think that made him a more effective witness for Christ? You bet it did. And he was honoring the Lord with his attitude and actions. As Proverbs says: "To do right honors God; to sin is to despise Him." (Proverbs 14:2 TLB) No matter what we say with our lips, if our conduct isn't right, we are demonstrating a lack of reverence and respect for the Lord, and we are damaging our witness.

Scripture says: "I, the Lord, search all hearts and examine secret motives. I give all people their due rewards, according to what their actions deserve." (Jeremiah 17:9-10 NLT) My husband had the right motives when he decided to help his company with their move, simply because it was the right thing to do. He wasn't being compensated for it by his company, and he wasn't even getting any special recognition. But he knew that the Lord saw his heart, and that He would honor his good intentions somehow. Besides that, Joe has always taken pride in his work, even when he was doing the most menial tasks. And he has always taken to heart the fact that, "Well-done work has its own reward." (Proverbs 12:14 MSG)

When the Bible talks about performing a job of any kind, it says, "Don't just do the minimum that will get you by. Do your best." (Colossians 3:23 MSG) In other words, do the job right. When Joe set about helping his company move, he threw all his energy into the task, and he did a good job. As he kept his eyes on the Lord, instead of on his employer or coworkers, he was able to resist the temptation to slack off or to feel sorry for himself. The rest of this scriptural passage says: "Work from the heart for your real Master, for God, confident that you'll get paid in full when you come into your inheritance. Keep in mind always that the ultimate Master you're serving is Christ. The sullen servant who does shoddy work will be held responsible. Being a follower of Jesus doesn't cover up bad work." (Colossians 3:23-25 MSG)

After my husband's company moved away, it was almost a year before he could find another job. During that time, he suffered a major heart attack, and we faced some serious financial problems. Would Joe have done things any differently when his company moved, had he known what troubles were up ahead for him? No. Because he did the right thing, simply because it was the right thing to do, he has had no regrets. And living without regret is a valuable reward in itself. Whatever you are facing today, will you answer God's call to do what is right in His sight, simply because it's the right thing to do?

Lord, please give me the courage, the strength, and the grace I need to do the right thing in every situation and circumstance without looking for a reward. Remind me often that my motives mean everything to You, and that no matter who I am dealing with, I am ultimately serving You. Thank You that as I concentrate on pleasing and glorifying You, I will live a life of satisfaction, fulfillment, and purpose!

Promise-Power Point: If I will honor the Lord by doing the right thing in every situation and circumstance, no matter how I am being treated, I will reap the heavenly and earthly rewards that cannot be received any other way.

People are Watching

"Our work as God's servants gets validated – or not – in the details. People are watching us as we stay at our post, alertly, unswervingly...in hard times, tough times, bad times." 2 Corinthians 6:4 MSG

A young woman wrote me and said that she feared that she had become a "stumbling block" to the young man she cared so deeply about. For a long time, she had tried to minister to this man, and to help him experience the love, forgiveness, and salvation of God. She desperately wanted to set a Christlike example for him, and to prove to him that not all Christians were "hypocrites," as he called them. Instead, she began spending more time with this man and his non-believing friends, and less time in Christian fellowship. She decided to be "less preachy, self-righteous, and judgmental," so that she could gain the acceptance of this new crowd, in order to become a "bridge" between them and Jesus. Eventually, she allowed this man to seduce her, and she said that since then, he has wanted nothing to do with her. As hurt as she was, she was most concerned that her sin would keep this young man from turning to the Lord. She feared that her ungodly behavior confirmed this man's suspicions about Christians, and about God Himself.

This young woman's experience made me think of some of the verses that address this very subject in the Bible. When the apostle Paul was speaking to some religious people of his day, he said: "You are so proud of knowing God's laws, but you dishonor Him by breaking them. No wonder the Scriptures say that the world speaks evil of God because of you." (Romans 2:23-24 TLB) Paul was trying to get across to these folks that their character and conduct were a reflection on the Lord, and the unbelieving world was closely watching them. That's why he instructed: "In everything set them an example by doing what is good...so that in every way, [you] will make the teaching about God our Savior attractive." (Titus 2:7, 10 NIV) The young woman who wrote me had the perfect opportunity to show the man she cared about that Jesus is real, and that His followers can be a lot like Him. Instead, she chose to compromise her walk with God, and to forfeit her chance to plant some seeds of faith in this man's life. Proverbs says: "If the godly compromise with the wicked, it is like polluting a fountain or muddying a spring." (Proverbs 25:26 NLT) Compromising Christians will not only have little impact on the world for Christ, but they can actually do more harm than good.

This woman's convictions were severely tested, but the Lord still expected her to do the right thing, considering He had equipped her with Holy Spirit power when she gave her life to Christ. The Bible is filled with Scriptures calling us to apply higher standards to our lives. Paul wrote: "We try to live in such a way that no one will be hindered from finding the Lord by the way we act, and so no one can find fault with our ministry. In everything we do we try to show that we are true ministers of God." (2 Corinthians 6:3-4 NLT) Scripture makes it abundantly clear that our conduct and the cause of Christ are closely linked, and the Lord expects us to act accordingly. The Message Bible says it this way: "Our work as God's servants gets validated – or not – in the details. People are watching us as we stay at our post, alertly, unswervingly...in hard times, tough times, bad times." (2 Corinthians 6:4) Because we are being watched at all times – by believers and non-believers alike – it's absolutely essential that we remain true to the Lord, His Word, and His ways. And we must be prepared to stand alone, and to be lonely, if the occasion calls for it. Just last night, my family went to the movies without me. I have lost count of all the times that this has happened because I hold myself to higher standards than most Christians do. I don't always like being left behind, but I have gotten the revelation that my choices affect other people, and that is what I try to focus on.

Maybe there are people in your life right now who you desperately want to lead to Christ. Perhaps you have already tried to speak to them about the message of the Gospel, and they have been unreceptive. The Scriptures reveal that setting a Christlike example can go a long way in reaching folks like these, when it says: "Your godly lives will speak to them better than any words." (1 Peter 3:2 TLB) Don't ever forget that God has equipped you with supernatural power to make a difference in this world. My advice to you today is straight from the Word of God – "Live wisely among those who are not Christians, and make the most of every opportunity"! (Colossians 4:5 NLT)

Lord, I regret all the times that I squandered precious opportunities You gave me to lead others into Your kingdom. Remind me often about these responsibilities and privileges of mine, as a believer in Christ. Thank You that as I strive to live like Jesus, You will use me to impact this world for all eternity!

Promise-Power Point: God has equipped me with Holy-Spirit power to touch and change lives for His glory, and He will use me to do exactly that when I am being led by His Spirit and His Word.

Our Spiritual Mentor

"I will ask the Father, and He will give you another Counselor to be with you forever – the Spirit of Truth."
John 14:16-17 NIV

Several months before my fortieth birthday, I went through some painful experiences that drove me to my knees in heartfelt prayer and repentance before God. I surrendered my heart and my life to the Lord for real that day, and it changed my life forever. I had been raised in the Christian faith, but had stopped going to church many years ago. I began watching some TV preachers and teachers, and listening to their Scripture-based messages. I realized almost immediately that God had planted a new hunger for His Word in my heart, and I began eagerly reading and studying the Bible for the first time in my life. Suddenly, the Lord seemed near to me, and I experienced His awesome presence like never before. I desperately wanted to get to know this God in an intimate way, so I invested in some good study Bibles, devotionals, and books filled with Scripture-based prayers. I had no church to rely on at the time, or to feed me with the Word of God, so I fed myself. My only "spiritual mentors" were the Bible teachers I watched on television, and the Holy Spirit Himself. As I look back, those were some of the sweetest times of fellowship with the Lord that I ever experienced, and I thank God for them.

Recently, I heard a story that reminded me of my early days of getting to know the Lord. It tells of a man who loved to study the Bible. Apparently, every time he came to something he didn't understand, he would ask his friend, Charlie, "What does this verse mean?" One day, in his Bible study time, the Holy Spirit asked him, "Why don't you ask Me? I'm the one who taught Charlie!" We hear a lot today about "spiritual mentors". Did you know that Jesus died so that you could have the best Spiritual Mentor in the world living on the inside of you every moment of every day? It's true. When Jesus told His disciples about His impending death, He said to them: "But I tell you the truth: It is for your good that I am going away. Unless I go away, the Counselor will not come to you; but if I go, I will send Him to you." (John 16:7 NIV) Another word for "counselor" is "mentor," and the Savior is speaking here of the Holy Spirit. Since Jesus paid such a terrible price so that His Spirit could teach and guide His followers continually, shouldn't we be making the most of this precious Gift?

The Lord also said: "But the Counselor, the Holy Spirit, whom the Father will send in My name, will teach you all things and will remind you of everything I have said to you." (John 14:26 NIV) Teachers and preachers can be extremely valuable in our walk with the Lord, but they are no substitute for the Spirit of

God. The Lord may use certain godly men and women to instruct and guide us at times, but He doesn't want us relying on these people in the same way that He desires us to depend on the leading of His Spirit. Many Christians today are out of God's will, and they are not fulfilling their God-given destiny, simply because they are listening to the wrong counsel, instead of following the leadership of the Holy Spirit.

If you have trusted Christ as your Savior, and have made Him the Lord of your life, then the Spirit of God lives in you, and you have the ability, the privilege, and the obligation to hear and heed God's voice. Each time you meet alone with the Lord with an open Bible and an open heart, you give Him the opportunity, not only to reveal Himself to you, but to help you fulfill your God-given purpose and potential, and to receive all the blessings and rewards He has in store for you. One way you can confirm that you are hearing from the Lord, is to make sure that the messages you are hearing are in agreement with the Word of God. It's the Holy Spirit who authored the Holy Scriptures, and He will never lead you to do something that contradicts God's Word. The God of the universe created you, has great plans for you, and wants to be intimately involved in your life. Will you do your part to get to know Him?

Lord, please show me how to rely more heavily on Your Spirit to mentor, teach, and guide me. Lead me to the right Bible study materials, and help me to set aside time to meet alone with You regularly. Thank You that as I do my part to get to know You better, You will help me to become all that You created me to be!

Promise-Power Point: I will receive clear guidance and instruction from the Spirit of God who dwells in me, as I submit to His leadership and listen for His voice.

The Question of Suffering

"Though He was God's Son, He learned trusting-obedience by what He suffered, just as we do." Hebrews 5:8 MSG

When I wrote about my husband's heart attack, and how the Lord mightily revealed His love and care throughout the whole ordeal, I heard from a woman who brought up some interesting questions. Wouldn't it have been an even bigger blessing, and a greater sign of God's love, if my husband hadn't had this heart attack in the first place? And if the Lord puts us through such tests to prove His greatness and power, doesn't that seem selfish on His part? I sympathized with this woman, because there have been plenty of times when I have had doubts of my own. But in the case of my husband's brush with death, all I could say was, "Thank You, Lord, for sparing my husband's life!" Should I have questioned God, and demanded answers from Him? No, because the Bible says that it pleases God when we find something to thank and praise Him for in every situation. I have discovered that if I make even a feeble attempt to find something good in a situation, I can always come up with something pretty quickly. Scripture says: "Thank [God] in everything [no matter what the circumstances may be; be thankful and give thanks], for this is the will of God for you [who are] in Christ Jesus." (1 Thessalonians 5:18 AMP)

I believe this woman missed a very important point on this subject – that God does not allow suffering to touch the lives of believers just to glorify Himself, but to equip His children to fulfill their God-given destinies. If you look at the people the Lord blessed and honored the most throughout the pages of the Bible, you will see that they were very often the ones who suffered the most. In fact, Scripture reveals that even Jesus was allowed to experience suffering, in order that He might fulfill His divine purpose here on earth. Hebrews 5:8-9 (NIV) says: "Although He was a Son, He learned obedience from what He suffered and, once made perfect, He became the source of eternal salvation for all who obey Him." Notice that it doesn't say that Jesus learned bitterness and resentment from His suffering, but He learned obedience instead. Each time that we experience testing times, we have to decide how we will respond. Those who humble themselves before the Lord, and seek to learn what it is He might want to teach them, will be rewarded in the end by a grateful God. One of these rewards will be spiritual growth and maturity. This Scripture says that Christ's suffering made Him "perfect". The Amplified version says it made Him "perfectly equipped". And the Message Bible uses the word "maturity". We are never going to experience the fullness of our God-given purpose while we are still spiritual babies. And the fact is that we do more growing and maturing in the hard times, than we do in the good times.

One of the things I love most about God is how He likes to turn our misery into ministry. A friend of mine was telling me the other day how one of her family members was pouring her heart out to her, and questioning God's intentions in allowing her to experience some painful trials. As a means of encouraging her heart, my friend told her of my husband's long-term unemployment, our oldest son's move across the country, and my husband's heart attack, and how the Lord allowed all these adversities, even though I had been serving Him with wholehearted devotion. As I listened to how God was already using my hurts and heartaches to console others, I became filled with an inexpressible joy. I would not have asked the Lord for the suffering I have endured, but neither can I resist thanking Him for how He is using it to touch and change lives. After all, how much of an impact does it make on others if we continue to love and serve God in the good times? But let them see us loving and serving the Lord with all our hearts in the midst of the storms of life, and they will not soon forget it.

We may not always understand how God operates, but those of us who have put our faith in Him know deep in our hearts that He is a good God, and He deserves our trust. Those who are able to rise above their own questions will experience the peace, joy, and contentment that Scripture promises. Today, lay hold of this divine guarantee that is yours in Christ: "[MOST] blessed is the man who believes in, trusts in, and relies on the Lord, and whose hope and confidence the Lord is"! (Jeremiah 17:7 AMP)

Lord, whenever I have questions or doubts, help me to take them straight to You. Show me how to experience Your love and concern, even in the midst of adversity. Remind me that Your matchless strength and comfort are available to me every moment of every day, just for the asking. Thank You that You can, and will, bring great good out of my hurt and heartache – for myself and for others! (Romans 8:28)

Promise-Power Point: *If I will believe and act as though God is a good God, and He will keep His promise to work all things for my good, I will experience Him lifting me above my circumstances, and using me to touch and change lives for His glory.*

No Pressure!

"If you do not stand firm in your faith, you will not stand at all." Isaiah 7:9 NIV

When our old sofa bed was about 20 years old, and no longer provided our overnight guests with a good night's sleep, my husband, Joe, and I went shopping for a new one. In the very first store we went to, we found a wonderful sofa bed that we thought was just what we were looking for. The best part was that we could have it delivered to our home in only one week's time, and we would have it before my sister and her husband came to visit us in two weeks. Even though I had already prayed that the Lord would help us make the right decision, I silently pleaded with Him once again – "Please don't let us do anything we are going to regret later, Lord." Suddenly, I sensed a lack of peace in my heart about buying this sofa bed. I turned to the saleslady and told her that I could not make a decision on the spot, and she began writing out a sales ticket for me, in the hope that I would come back and purchase it at a later time. Joe knew that I had been only one second away from buying that sofa bed, so he asked me what had changed my mind. I told him, "After I prayed about it, I realized that I didn't have peace about it, and I felt that we should wait." As we left the store, I noticed that right across the street was a furniture store that sold the same brand as our bedroom set. Joe and I both agreed that we should check it out. As soon as we saw the sofa beds they offered, we knew that we had done the right thing by delaying our decision in the first store. We were going to have to wait eight weeks to get our new sofa bed, but we were sure it would be worth it because of the high quality of the product, and the peace we had in our hearts as we placed the order.

This pleasant experience reminded me of one that my husband and I had several years earlier that didn't end so pleasantly. Joe's old car had died, and we knew that we had to replace it quickly, so we began searching used car lots in our area. We found what we thought was the perfect car, but the price was higher than we could afford. When my husband asked the salesman if he could come down in price, the man flatly refused. As we began leaving the car lot, the salesman stopped us and said, "If you buy this car right now, I will throw in the warranty for free." Joe couldn't resist the offer, and he said without thinking, "You've got a deal!" The very first day my husband was driving his new car to work, the engine blew up. He was furious, because he was sure that we had been swindled. Even so, he knew it would have been much worse if we didn't have the warranty on the car, which helped to pay for most of the repair expenses.

Why did these two shopping experiences end so differently? Because even though my husband and I sought the Lord's wisdom and guidance in both of them, we only followed His Spirit's leading in one of them. When we went shopping for a car, instead of yielding to the promptings of the Holy Spirit, we yielded to the pressures of a salesman. How often do we miss out on God's best because we allow ourselves to be pressured into doing things that are out of His will for us? Scripture says: "If you need wisdom – if you want to know what God wants you to do – ask Him, and He will gladly tell you." (James 1:5 NLT) Notice it says that the Lord will gladly tell us what to do when we ask Him to. It doesn't say that He will twist our arms and force us into doing what is best for us. But there WILL be people in this world who will have no qualms about pushing us and pressuring us into doing what THEY want us to do. If we don't stand strong in times of pressure, we will never fulfill the call of God on our lives, and we will live our lives in mediocrity and frustration. The Bible says: "The people who know their God shall prove themselves strong and shall stand firm and do exploits [for God]". (Daniel 11:32 AMP) I have discovered that the closer I get to the Lord, the easier it is for me to stand firm against this kind of pressure, and the more He uses me and promotes me for His glory. My heartfelt prayer for you today is that you would grow strong in the Lord, until you are able to resist the pressure that would rob you of His best!

Lord, forgive me for the times I caved in to the pressure that others put on me to do and be what wasn't Your will for me. Make me strong in You, and help me to do my part by wholly devoting myself to You and Your Word. Thank You that as I learn to stand firm, I will reap the very best of your blessings every time!

Promise-Power Point: The world, the flesh, and the devil will not be able to rob me of God's best as long as I am drawing on His wisdom and strength for every situation and circumstance of life.

Winning Battles God's Way

"Do not say, 'I'll pay you back for this wrong!' Wait for the Lord, and He will deliver you." Proverbs 20:22 NIV

It seems that one of the hardest things for us to do is to wait for God to deliver us when we are victims of wrongdoing. Often our first reaction is to become angry or offended, or to retaliate somehow. Unfortunately, when we do that, we usually forfeit any help we might have gotten from the Lord. God taught me something about this through a painful lesson some years ago.

My husband and I had just moved into our new home in Eastern Pennsylvania, and our two young sons began to get acquainted with the other kids in the neighborhood. At first, we were delighted that our children were making new friends, but it wasn't too long before we realized that these neighborhood kids were often mischievous, and even malicious. Things got so bad that my husband and I finally told our sons that they were no longer allowed to associate with the neighborhood gang. We were as gracious about this as possible, but our neighbors became offended, and their children began threatening our kids and attacking our home and property, doing some serious damage. When trying to reason with these kids and their parents didn't work, we resorted to calling on the police for help. Not only did that fail to work, but it actually made the problem – and the attacks – worse.

All this time, I prayed and stood on God's promises for deliverance, while my husband became more and more bitter, and contemplated taking matters into his own hands. Then one night, we caught one of the troublesome kids red-handed, and we filed charges against him. His parents came to my husband late that night, pleading with him to drop the charges against their son. I was amazed when my husband agreed and sent that family home, relieved and grateful. The police were not pleased with my husband's decision. They warned us that we had given up our only chance to stop the attacks on our home and family. But since that night, we have lived here in peace. In addition, the Lord restored our home by causing our insurance company to put all new siding on our house.

Since then, whenever my family and I encounter injustice of any kind, we seek God's direction, and we depend on Him to vindicate us. Yes, there are times we may have to take appropriate action – perhaps even legal action – but it should only be at God's direction and with His approval. Otherwise, it will be futile, or even disastrous. If you are in need of deliverance from injustice today, be encouraged by God's promise to you – "The Lord will vindicate His people and have compassion on His servants." (Psalm 135:14 NIV)

Lord, when I am a victim of injustice, help me to seek Your direction above everyone else's. Show me when to take appropriate action, and when to wait on You for deliverance. Guard me from being easily offended, angered, or vindictive. Teach me how to let You fight my battles for me so that I can gain the victory every time. Remind me that taking matters into my own hands can have disastrous results. Thank You for promising to be my Vindicator and my Defender! (Isaiah 54:17; Luke 18:7-8)

Promise-Power Point: Because of my faith in Christ, God will fight all of my battles when I surrender them to Him, and cooperate with His plans for my deliverance and victory.

The Best Lesson My Dad Ever Taught Me

"Let everyone see that you are unselfish and considerate in all you do." Philippians 4:5 TLB

There are a lot of Thanksgiving Day memories that have remained with me over the years, but the ones that I treasure most were made on this holiday in the year 1990. My husband and I, and our two young sons, were having Thanksgiving dinner at my parents' house, along with all of my sisters and their families. As usual, we were eating an abundance of rich foods, and making merry. When dinner was over, and we began clearing off the table, my father approached my sisters and me with a somber expression on his face. As he began sharing with us how our grandmother, his own mother, had died that very morning, my sisters and I burst into tears. "Granny" had lived with us the entire time we were growing up. She had been like a second mother to us, and we loved her dearly. In recent years, her health had declined to the point that she had to be moved into a nursing home, but she was still a very big part of our family. I must confess that when I first realized that my dad had delayed in telling us the sad news, I was angry. But after my emotions settled down, I began to recognize what a selfless act of love he had performed. He knew the depth of the love we felt for our grandmother, and he wanted us to have some time rejoicing together as a family, before he had to break the unpleasant news to us. Many years later, I still marvel at the precious gift my father presented to all of us that day.

The Bible says: "Each of you should look not only to your own interests, but also to the interests of others. Your attitude should be the same as that of Christ Jesus..." (Philippians 2:4-5 NIV) I can't help thinking of these verses when I think about what my dad did that Thanksgiving Day years ago. And I have often asked myself if I could ever have done such a thing. Quite honestly, I doubt it. I was brought up in a generation that was called the "Me Generation," and with good reason. We were always told, "Look out for number one." And, "If you don't look out for yourself, no one will." So when I began studying the Scriptures in earnest, it shocked my senses to discover that God expected me to look out for other people's interests as much as my own, or even more so. At first, I was intimidated by the "love commands" that I found in the Bible, but then I realized that God had equipped me with everything I needed to succeed in this area. Scripture says: "Now you can have real love for everyone because your souls have been cleansed from selfishness and hatred when you trusted Christ to save you; so see to it that you really do love each other warmly, with all your hearts." (1 Peter 1:22 TLB) When we received Christ as our personal Savior, His Spirit came to dwell in us, and to continually pour the God-kind of love into our hearts. (Romans 5:5) But living a life of love is still a choice that we have to make on a moment-by-moment basis. The world, our own flesh, and the devil will try to keep us focused on ourselves. By giving our relationship with God first place in our life – and making prayer, praise, and Bible study a priority – we can cooperate with the Lord to become more Christlike every day.

If you had asked me years ago if I was a selfish person, I would have answered with an emphatic, "No". That was before I got serious about my relationship with the Lord, and about studying His Word. I was judging myself by the world's standards, not God's. Once I discovered what His standards were, I realized that I had been living a very selfish lifestyle, and that I needed to change. One of the first things I noticed was that my level of joy increased immeasurably. Seek out a truly self-centered individual, and you will find a truly miserable person. On the other hand, look for someone who is living a lifestyle of giving to others – of their time, talents, and treasure – and you will undoubtedly discover someone who enjoys a sense of contentment. The Bible says: "The one who blesses others is abundantly blessed; those who help others are helped." (Proverbs 11:25 MSG) The truth is, we can't be a blessing to others without being blessed ourselves. My dad has since gone to be with the Lord, but he left me a gift and a legacy that lives on to bless me and my loved ones. And if he were here today, he would give you some valuable advice straight from the Word of God – "Don't think only of yourself. Try to think of the other fellow, too, and what is best for him"! (1 Corinthians 10:24 TLB)

Lord, when I am feeling joyless and empty inside, remind me to check my "selfish level". Do such a mighty work in me that everyone will see that I am unselfish and considerate in all I do. (Philippians 4:5 TLB) Thank You that my selfless lifestyle will touch and change lives for Your glory!

Promise-Power Point: *No matter what my circumstances are, I can live a joyful and fulfilling life when I cheerfully consider others above myself according to God's will.*

The Humble Get the Help

"As the Scriptures say, 'God sets Himself against the proud, but He shows favor to the humble.'" James 4:6 NLT

My husband, Joe, taught us all a wonderful lesson in humility one evening when he was driving home from work, and was tired and anxious to get home. Even though he knew better than to drive too fast, he threw caution aside, and leaned on the accelerator. As soon as he saw the flashing lights of a police car coming up behind him, he immediately turned to the Lord, and humbly asked for His forgiveness and help. When the police officer approached Joe and chastised him for driving so recklessly, my husband admitted his wrongdoing and guilt without hesitation. As a result, the officer did not slap Joe with the severe penalty he deserved, but gave him instead a minor fine, and sent him on his way. Overjoyed and grateful, my husband thanked the officer and gave praise to God, vowing to be more careful in the future.

This experience is a perfect example of the truth of James 4:6 (NLT), which says: "God sets Himself against the proud, but He shows favor to the humble." Time and time again, my family and I have witnessed the difference it makes in our lives and circumstances when we have resisted being prideful and stubborn, and have chosen to humble ourselves before God and others. I can remember a time when my husband would be in exactly the same situation as I just described, but instead of reacting with humility, he would react with anger and stubborn pride. Needless to say, the results were always negative, and sometimes the consequences were even devastating. Once my husband began resisting the temptation to become hostile or offended in situations like these, he began experiencing for himself the goodness of God. Now he is "hooked" and knows that when he's in a "tight spot," the best thing for him to do is to humbly admit his fault, and pray for the Lord's forgiveness and help. Why don't more people experience for themselves the goodness of God? The answer is simple – pride. While the Lord earnestly desires to reveal His goodness to us, He can't do that as long as pride is controlling our lives. That's why Satan works overtime trying to get us to become offended, angry, and willful. He knows that these attitudes can drive a wedge between us and God. They can keep us from enjoying the fullness of God's blessings, and can ultimately prevent us from fulfilling our God-given purpose.

Suppose when that police officer pulled my husband over that day, he thought to himself, "I was wrong and I don't deserve the Lord's help, so I won't expect it or ask for it." This is another mistake that so many of us make. We get caught doing wrong, and we decide for ourselves that we don't deserve God's mercy or assistance, so we don't ask for them. This is just as wrong as reacting with anger or hostility. First Peter 5:6-7 (TLB) says: "If you will humble yourselves under the mighty hand of God, in His good time He will lift you up. Let Him have all your worries and cares, for He is always thinking about you and watching everything that concerns you." The Lord longs to have us humbly turn to Him in our times of need, so that He can demonstrate His unconditional love for us, and His willingness to act on our behalf. When we make a mistake, God isn't going to make us feel worse by beating us over the head with guilt and condemnation. That's the devil's job. Today, my heartfelt prayer for you is that the next time you are in a "tight spot," you will remember that it's the humble that get God's help!

Lord, forgive me for the times I've been prideful, angry, or willful – instead of humble, reasonable, and cooperative. From now on when I'm in trouble, remind me to seek Your help and forgiveness, even when I don't deserve them. Give me the grace I need to grow and mature in Christ, and help me to do my part in the process. Thank You for revealing Your goodness and love to me in awesome new ways!

Promise-Power Point: God is infinitely merciful, and He will show me His mercy in extraordinary ways when I turn to Him in heartfelt repentance and humility.

Skills Blessed by God

"Bless all his skills, O Lord, and be pleased with the work of his hands." Deuteronomy 33:11 NIV

This is a prayer-promise that I stand on almost every day for myself and my loved ones. When I get into my car, I pray, "Bless all my driving skills, O Lord, and be pleased with the work of my hands." I want God's help to make me a safe, skillful, and responsible driver, especially when I have passengers in my car. I also pray and apply this promise to my writing and ministry skills. I not only want the Lord to give me supernatural skills, but I also want to speak and write in ways that please Him most.

When my sister was having the front steps of her house completely reconstructed, she was understandably concerned, and she asked for my prayers. I shared with her the scriptural prayer above, and I encouraged her to pray it on behalf of the men who would be doing the work on her house. She did exactly that, and when I saw her new front steps, I was amazed at the extraordinary skills and efforts that must have been involved to produce such beautiful results.

The Scriptures make it clear that God wants us to ask Him to be involved in all our efforts, not just so that they will succeed, but so that they will please and glorify Him. Proverbs 3:4-6 (TLB) reads: "Trust the Lord completely; don't ever trust yourself. In everything you do, put God first, and He will direct you, and crown your efforts with success." I know from experience that this promise can be applied to everything we do, including our food preparation. I am "famous" for my manicotti, my deviled eggs, and my apple crumb pie because before I begin them, I pray and claim this promise as my own, trusting the Lord to guide and bless my efforts. And I believe that it honors Him when others are blessed by my culinary skills.

When God created you, He gave you skills and gifts that are unlike anyone else's. He not only wants you to ask Him what they are, but He also wants you to seek Him for His divine blessing upon them. When you do, you will touch the lives of others, and give Him great glory!

Lord, reveal to me the special gifts and skills that You have blessed me with. Show me how to do my part to perfect them and make them more valuable all the time. I want to use them for the good of others, Lord, as well as for Your glory. Today, I choose to invite You into all of my work, and to seek Your blessing on all that I do!

Promise-Power Point: When I commit my work to God, and ask for His guidance and blessing, He will cause my efforts to succeed and prosper in ways that honor Him most.

Spiritual Smokescreens

"Take your stand against the devil's schemes." Ephesians 6:11 NIV

Once we trust Christ as our Savior and are filled with the Holy Spirit, the devil has no authority or jurisdiction over us. Even so, he can still have a tremendous influence on our lives by using the weapon of deception. And one of his most devastating tools is "spiritual smokescreens". Let me give you a classic example of how Satan uses these tactics, so that you can be on your guard against them.

Years ago, my husband, Joe, and I had some serious problems with our neighbors' children, who intimidated our sons and did significant damage to our house and property. Ever since then, my husband has been overly sensitive to apparent attacks on our home. The devil is keenly aware of this, and he does his best to use it against our family. One Saturday, when our mail lady delivered our mail, she asked my husband if he ever found out who had tied explosives to our above-the-ground pool and tried to blow it up. This incident happened two years previous, so her question seemed to come out of the blue. When my husband had to admit that we never did discover the culprit, she said, "You have some bad kids in this neighborhood." This was the first step that Satan took in creating a spiritual smokescreen against my family.

Next, during the wee hours of that very night, my husband was awakened by a very loud bang. He jumped out of bed, and heard voices whispering, and then feet fleeing, and he was convinced that whoever it was, was up to no good. Satan was setting my husband up, to get him upset.

Then, the following morning, Joe went outside to look for any signs of damage to our home or property. He came to me sometime later, holding huge branches which he said someone must have ripped from our trees. I told him sternly, "Now don't go looking for trouble where there is none." After closer inspection, Joe discovered that the broken branches were from a tree down the road that belonged to a neighbor who was having work done to his property, and that no attack had been made on us after all.

The devil uses spiritual smokescreens to make things look much worse than they really are. If we're sick, Satan will try to convince us that we're not going to get any better. If we're having financial problems, he'll try to make us think that we are going to lose everything. If we're experiencing relationship troubles, he will attempt to convince us that we are going to be rejected. If we don't commit our situation to God, and trust Him for His protection and help, we will buy into the devil's lies, and rob ourselves of the blessings that the Lord had in store for us. The Bible says that we are to be on guard at all times, "so that no advantage would be taken of us by Satan, for we are not ignorant of his schemes". (2 Corinthians 2:11 NASB) If my husband had not become aware of the devil's tactics in his situation, he would have acted rashly and opened the door to all kinds of trouble. Thankfully, he eventually saw through the enemy's schemes, and he refused to take the devil's bait.

The next time you are faced with what could be a spiritual smokescreen, turn to the Lord immediately in prayer, and ask for His discernment and help. Claim His promises for protection and provision, and praise Him for His faithfulness. Take any appropriate, practical steps that the Lord leads you to take. Then rest in the peace and security that belong to you in Christ!

Lord, teach me how to be alert for spiritual smokescreens. Give me the supernatural wisdom and discernment I need to recognize them the moment they come my way. Remind me often that Satan is always working overtime to make things look worse than they really are. Thank You that as I stand against the strategies of the devil, and put my trust in You, I will gain the victory each and every time!

Promise-Power Point: God has equipped me to see through the enemy's spiritual smokescreens, and I will avoid the devil's traps when I live a Christ-centered life, and seek Him daily for His guidance and grace.

Getting Burned

"Can a man scoop fire into his lap and not be burned?" Proverbs 6:27 NLT

I recently heard from a lady who asked for prayer for a mate. She said that she had been waiting many years for someone to love her, and that she had been "burned" twice. She told me, "God gave to me, and then took away, and left me with unbearable pain." While I sympathized with this woman, I knew she needed more than pity – she needed some words of wisdom. So after I earnestly prayed for her, I did my best to offer her some godly counsel.

I told this lady that if she had been "burned twice," then she had undoubtedly been involved with relationships that were not from God. The Bible says, "Can a man hold fire against his chest and not be burned?" (Proverbs 6:27 TLB) When we play with wrong relationships, we are playing with fire, and we WILL get burned. And though we shouldn't blame God when we don't like the results we get from our disobedience, we often do this very thing. As Proverbs says, "People ruin their lives by their own foolishness and then are angry at the Lord." (Proverbs 19:3 NLT) Blaming God for failed relationships that were not His will to begin with will get us nowhere. God is not our problem. He doesn't send us friends or mates that will abuse us, lie to us, or torment us. Or who will discourage our wholehearted devotion to Him. If we will let Him, the Lord will send us companions who will love us with the God-kind of love, who will bring out the best in us, and who will help us become all that God created us to be. As the Bible assures us, "Every good and perfect gift is from above, coming down from the Father of the heavenly lights, who does not change like shifting shadows." (James 1:17 NIV)

A biblical principle that will keep us out of a lot of trouble is Proverbs 28:26 (NIV): "He who trusts in himself is a fool, but he who walks in wisdom is kept safe." When we allow ourselves to get involved in relationships that are outside of God's will, we step out from under His "safety umbrella". And we expose ourselves to misery and heartache that the Lord never meant us to suffer. Proverbs warns: "Above all else, guard your affections. For they influence everything else in your life." (Proverbs 4:23 TLB) Our relationships will determine the course of our lives. Satan is keenly aware of this fact, and that is exactly why he works overtime trying to tempt us with wrong relationships. If this is a weakness of ours, he will continually torment us in this area.

One of the main things I discerned from this troubled lady's letter was that she had a tendency to be what Scripture calls "double-minded". (James 1:7 NIV) The Bible addresses this problem when it encourages us to seek the Lord for His wisdom in matters that concern us. "But when you ask Him, be sure that your faith is in God alone. Do not waver, for a person with divided loyalty is as unsettled as a wave of the sea that is blown and tossed by the wind. Such people should not expect to receive anything from the Lord. Their loyalty is divided between God and the world, and they are unstable in everything they do." (James 1:6-8 NLT) Clearly, this woman's loyalty was divided. Or as one translation says, she was "keeping all of [her] options open." (James 1:8 MSG) Rather than waiting for the Lord to send her "Mr. Right," she was settling for "Mr. Right Now". She was saying to the Lord, "Instead of trusting and leaning on You, I am just going to lean on 'Mr. Wrong' for a while, till You decide to send me 'Mr. Right.'" But as God's Word says, "Don't think you're going to get anything from the Master that way!" (James 1:8 MSG)

When we are suffering loneliness or heartache because we lack a godly mate or friends, we must be very careful not to focus on our needs and desires in this area, but to keep our focus on the Lord. Jesus commanded us to seek first God's kingdom and righteousness, and He meant it. (Matthew 6:33) If He is not given first place in our lives to begin with, He is not likely to provide us with companions who will distract us even more from loving Him with all of our hearts, souls, minds, and strength. (Luke 10:27) Once we make up our minds that Jesus is all we will ever need – and we prove it by our actions for a season – He will send us all the companionships we need to live the rich, full lives He has called us to!

Lord, forgive me for the times I settled for wrong relationships because I wasn't willing to wait on You for Your best. Give me the grace I need to endure seasons of loneliness, if necessary, in order to do Your will in this area. Thank You that as I determine to walk in wisdom, and to give You first place in my life, You will send me the perfect companions at the perfect time!

Promise-Power Point: It is not God's will for me to get burned by wrong relationships, and if I will set my heart on pleasing Him in this area, He will send me only companions who will bring out the best in me, and encourage my devotion to Him.

Small Beginnings

"Do not despise these small beginnings, for the Lord rejoices to see the work begin." Zechariah 4:10 NLT

Years ago, I read a true story about the humble beginnings of one of the most famous composers of all time. It told of how this composer rose to greatness, and ended up touching countless lives, by simply preparing music for the Sunday services at his church each week. At the time that I read this amazing story, I was feeling very discouraged and disheartened in my work for the Lord. Reading about this man's devotion and dedication inspired me and encouraged my heart. I had been laboring in the Lord's name for many years, and had received little recognition or reward. I often asked myself questions like, "Where are the blessings? Where are my rewards?" I eventually discovered that the thing that helped me most was to shift my focus from, "What's in it for me?" to "How can I help others?"

The Bible clearly states that God's people will be richly rewarded for loving and serving Him. But it doesn't say WHEN we will be rewarded, or even how. One reason for this is that God doesn't want us focusing on our rewards, but on doing the work He has assigned us to do while we are on this earth. And He expects us to perform our work faithfully. Jesus said, "He who is faithful in a very little thing is faithful also in much." (Luke 16:10 NASB) Before the Lord entrusts us with big assignments, He tests us in smaller ones. Some people aren't interested in doing seemingly insignificant tasks for God. What they don't realize is that God may never allow them to do great things for Him, unless they are first willing to do humble tasks, and to prove themselves trustworthy.

In my case, God had called me to be a prayer intercessor. As I proved myself faithful in this capacity, He led me to begin writing devotionals. As I concentrated on preparing my devotional newsletter each week, the Lord opened a door for my work to be published in book form. As it turned out, I was in ministry many years before I received any monetary reward. Even now, most of my work is done on a strictly volunteer basis. And, frankly, I worry about Christians who have very little interest in serving the Lord without pay. Yes, it's true that the Bible is filled with promises of prosperity and reward for those who love and serve God. But most of the time, we will have to do the right thing for a long time, before we get the right results.

Scripture says, "Do not despise these small beginnings, for the Lord rejoices to see the work begin." (Zechariah 4:10 NLT) When God leads us to start out small in our service for Him, we mustn't look down on our humble beginnings. If you look at the people the Lord used most throughout the centuries, you will see that even the greatest of these started out small. One of these was the apostle Paul himself. He wrote, "I thank Christ Jesus our Lord, who has strengthened me, because He considered me faithful, putting me into service." (1 Timothy 1:12 NASB) As we prove ourselves faithful in each assignment the Lord gives us, He will reward us with greater opportunities to serve Him. Paul went through some incredibly hard times during his years of ministry, but he fiercely fought against the urge to quit and give up, and he inspired others to do the same. He said, "Since God has so generously let us in on what He is doing, we're not about to throw up our hands and walk off the job just because we run into occasional hard times." (2 Corinthians 4:1 MSG)

One of the promises from God that has kept me going in the toughest of times is Hebrews 6:10 (NIV): "God is not unjust; He will not forget your work and the love you have shown Him as you have helped His people and continue to help them." The Lord is a just and righteous God, and He is committed to seeing that His people are rewarded and recognized for their work and devotion to Him. As one godly man put it, "The rewards for doing right are sometimes delayed, but they are guaranteed by God Himself." I still get discouraged in my work for the Lord sometimes, but now when I do, I just focus on the little things, helping one person at a time. If you are struggling with "small beginnings" today, I pray that this precious promise from God will be an encouragement to you – "Your beginnings will seem humble, so prosperous will your future be"! (Job 8:7 NIV)

Lord, when I am tempted to look down on the work You assign to me, help me to shift my focus from myself to You and others. When discouragement comes against me, remind me to look to You for encouragement and strength. Thank You that as I prove myself faithful in little things, You will not only promote me, but You will make me a world-changer for Your glory!

Promise-Power Point: If I will refuse to give in to discouragement and despair when my work for God brings me little recognition or reward, I will eventually receive all the blessings that only a faithful servant of the Lord can enjoy.

Reasoning Away His Blessings

"I am the Lord; that is My name! I will not give My glory to anyone else, nor share My praise..." Isaiah 42:8 NLT

When the Lord miraculously delivered my husband, Joe, from a large growth in his neck, we began hearing other people's "take" on the situation. Listening to others trying to reason this miracle away was sometimes frustrating and bewildering. I confess that there were times when my husband and I were tempted to fall victim to their skepticism and doubts. Knowing this, the Lord sent us some very special encouragement through our neighbor across the street. He stopped by one day to bring us fresh greens to feed our pet ducks. When I asked how his wife was doing, he said that she was recovering from surgery to remove a cancerous growth from her neck. His description of his wife's malady was almost identical to my husband's in every way. The only difference was that her growth did not miraculously disappear, but it remained and had become cancerous. I knew that this man's visit to my home at just the right time was not a coincidence. It was God's way of highlighting the wonders He worked on my husband's behalf in response to our praying in faith for a miracle, and standing on His Word.

The Bible says: "Call on Me when you are in trouble, and I will rescue you, and you will give Me glory." (Psalm 50:15 NLT) Unfortunately, many people – including Christians – act as though this verse reads: "Call upon Me when you are in trouble, and I will rescue you, and you shall rationalize away all My blessings." What amazes me most is that many of the believers who fervently prayed for Joe during his ordeal were suspicious and doubtful of the miracle that God performed on his behalf – partly in response to their own prayers! This not only grieves the heart of God, but it deeply offends Him, too. The Lord spoke through Isaiah the prophet saying, "I will not yield My glory to another." (Isaiah 48:11 NIV) God is not about to share His glory with anyone, and He expects to get the credit when He acts.

In the first chapter of Romans, the apostle Paul records some chilling descriptions of those who reject the one true God. Romans 1:21 (AMP) reads: "When they knew and recognized Him as God, they did not honor and glorify Him as God or give Him thanks. But instead they became futile and godless in their thinking [with vain imaginings, foolish reasoning, and stupid speculations] and their senseless minds were darkened." Notice that these people did not give God the glory due Him, and they refused to give Him the thanks He deserved. Instead, they engaged in "foolish reasoning." Sadly, there are many believers who do this very thing, when they let worldly mindsets and attitudes creep into their minds and hearts. The good news is that we don't have to give place to ungodly thoughts or beliefs. Instead, we can cast down "arguments and theories and reasonings and every proud and lofty thing that sets itself up against the [true] knowledge of God." And we can "lead every thought and purpose away captive into the obedience of Christ." (2 Corinthians 10:5 AMP) And that's exactly what God expects His children to do – every single time.

One of the best ways to cut off the flow of God's blessings into our lives is to reason away His blessings. On the other hand, giving God the thanks and the praise for every one of His gifts – both large and small – will keep the door open to His involvement in our lives. My husband's healing and deliverance had God's signature all over it, and no matter how others try to explain it away, I am determined to give Him all the glory. What gift from above can YOU give Him thanks and praise for today?

Lord, forgive me for all of the times You acted on my behalf in a time of need, and I failed to give You the glory. I confess it as sin, and I ask that You do a new work in me, so that I might recognize and acknowledge Your intimate involvement in my life from now on. Thank You for all that You have done for me in the past, and for all that You will do for me in the days to come!

Promise-Power Point: As I refuse to reason away God's blessings and opportunities in my life, and as I acknowledge and give thanks for all His goodness on my behalf, I will keep the door open for Him to reveal Himself to me more and more.

God's Antidote for Disappointment

"I am the Lord; those who hope in Me will not be disappointed." Isaiah 49:23 NIV

I once saw a famous baseball player talking about his faith on television. He spoke about how placing our confidence in people was a mistake, and how we should only put our hope in God. In fact, he made a startling statement like, "People will let us down 100 percent of the time, but God will never let us down." If I had heard this man talking like this before I became a committed Christian years ago, I might have thought he was being terribly cynical. But now I know better. The Bible says, "It is better to trust the Lord than to put confidence in people." (Psalm 118:8 NLT) The truth is, whenever we put our confidence in people, or become dependent upon them for our needs, we will be disappointed. Only God can make the statement – "Those who hope in Me will not be disappointed" – and have it hold true. (Isaiah 49:23 NIV) Jesus did not have a cynical or suspicious nature, and yet He did not put His confidence in people. Scripture says: "But Jesus didn't trust them, because He knew what people were really like. No one needed to tell Him about human nature." (John 2:24-25 NLT) Jesus loved people enough to die for them, but His faith and hope were in God, not in man. We need to follow His example. (1 Peter 1:21)

Years ago, I heard a godly man say that whenever we compromise God's Word to gain or keep something or someone, we will lose what we are trying to hold on to. I have learned the hard way that there is a lot of truth to that statement. If you are involved in a relationship that is not God's best for you, and you turn your back on the Lord's will to please this person, you will either watch them slip away from you no matter what you do, or what is sweet between you now will eventually become sour. Even when we are in God's perfect will relationship-wise, we will face disappointment regularly. So why would we want to be involved with a relationship that wasn't God's best for us? If our confidence and hope are properly placed in God, HE will fulfill all our needs and desires. Even when the Lord uses others to meet some of our needs, we are not to become dependent upon these people, or to place our confidence in them. While we should appreciate them, we should depend only upon God.

Some believers compromise their Christian values because they are afraid of being alone. But those fears are unfounded because God has promised to provide ALL our needs if we let Him, and that includes our social and emotional needs. Jesus knew better than anyone what it was like to be disappointed and alone. Just before He went to the cross He said to His disciples: "The time is coming – in fact, it is already here – when you will be scattered, each one going his own way, leaving Me alone. Yet I am not alone because the Father is with Me." (John 16:32 NLT) Jesus knew that even if all of His loved ones deserted Him, His Heavenly Father would still be there for Him. That's a message for all of us to take to heart. Today, it is my earnest prayer that you will put your wholehearted trust in the only One who can ever truthfully say – "I will never, never fail you nor forsake you!" (Hebrews 13:15 TLB)

Lord, right now, I commit myself to You and ask You to bring me into the center of Your will in every area of my life. Don't let me compromise my relationship with You to please myself or others. When others disappointment me, I ask that You comfort me and remind me that Your presence and provision are always available to me. Thank You that because my hope is in You, I won't be disappointed!

Promise-Power Point: If I refuse to misplace my trust, and keep it firmly and consistently in the Lord, I will experience His mighty intervention whenever I am in need.

Battle Scars

"The Scriptures tell us that for His sake we must be ready to face death at every moment of the day – we are like sheep awaiting slaughter; but despite all this, overwhelming victory is ours through Christ who loved us enough to die for us." Romans 8:36-37 TLB

I had started making some real progress in overcoming some bad habits that had plagued me for years – and that I knew were keeping me from experiencing God's best plans for my life – when I got hit with a severe attack on my health. As I stood on God's promises for deliverance and healing, I got hit with another debilitating attack. I finally went to the Lord and pressed Him for answers. "What's going on here, Lord? I feel like I'm finally doing what You want me to, and now this happens. I don't get it." That's when He led me to Psalm 44. Here, the psalmist shares his bewilderment with his God. He and his people have been faithful to the Lord, yet they are being attacked, defeated, and disgraced at every turn. By the time he gets to the end of the psalm, it dawns on him that he is suffering precisely BECAUSE he is committed to the Lord. He writes: "Yet for YOUR SAKE we face death all day long; we are considered as sheep to be slaughtered." (Psalm 44:22 NIV) In other words, the psalmist's suffering was not divine chastisement, but a battle scar as a result of his devotion and commitment to the Lord.

The apostle Paul quotes this same verse in the book of Romans. "The Scriptures tell us that for His sake we must be ready to face death at every moment of the day – we are like sheep awaiting slaughter; but despite all this, overwhelming victory is ours through Christ who loved us enough to die for us." (Romans 8:36-37 TLB) The Bible doesn't try to deceive us. It tells us plainly that when we make the decision to live for God, we must be prepared to suffer because of that decision. Paul wrote: "For to you has been given the privilege not only of trusting Him but also of suffering for Him. We are in this fight together." (Philippians 1:29-30 TLB) If we don't take Scriptures like these to heart, the next time we face suffering, we will automatically think that we have done something wrong. But the truth is that, for a believer, suffering can be a sign of loyalty. The apostle Peter wrote: "For God called you to do good, even if it means suffering, just as Christ suffered for you. He is your example, and you must follow in His steps." (1 Peter 2:21 NLT) Peter knew from personal experience that doing good often led to suffering. And he reminds us that Jesus Himself suffered greatly in many ways because of His obedience, and we are to follow His example.

You and I need to keep in mind that we have the same enemies that Jesus did – Satan and his evil forces. As Scripture says: "We are not fighting against flesh-and-blood enemies, but against evil rulers and authorities of the unseen world, against mighty powers in this dark world, and against evil spirits in the heavenly places."

(Ephesians 6:12 NLT) Much of our suffering will come from the devil's attempts to tempt, accuse, and deceive us, so we must be on guard at all times. As Peter says: "Be careful – watch out for attacks from Satan, your great enemy. He prowls around like a hungry, roaring lion, looking for some victim to tear apart. Stand firm when he attacks. Trust the Lord; and remember that other Christians all around the world are going through these sufferings too." (1 Peter 5:8-9 TLB) One of the things that comforts me most when I am hurting is that I am not being singled out to suffer, but my brothers and sisters in Christ everywhere are undergoing their own trials, and they can relate to my struggles.

When we are suffering in some way, we should ask the Lord to show us anything we might have done to open a door to satanic attack. If He doesn't show us anything, it might be wise to consider the fact that we are being attacked because of our faithfulness, not our unfaithfulness. We must remind ourselves that if God allows adversity to touch our lives, then He has a divine purpose for it, and He will cause it to profit us somehow. (Romans 8:28) Believing and acting on these truths will spare us from having to reap the penalty of a wrong response to our trials. If you are hurting today, I invite you to – "Take [with me] your share of the hardships and suffering [which you are called to endure] as a good (first-class) soldier of Christ Jesus"! (2 Timothy 2:3 AMP)

Lord, when I am under attack in some way, remind me that what Satan meant for my harm, You will work for my good, as long as I am trusting in You. (Genesis 50:20) Help me to devote myself to prayer and Your Word, so that I can "be firm in faith," as You have called me to be. (1 Peter 5:8 AMP) Thank You for the "overwhelming victory" that is mine through Christ who loves me! (Romans 8:37)

Promise-Power Point: When trouble strikes, I will go to God for discernment and clarity, and He will equip me to respond to my trials in ways that will profit me most in the long run.

Give Him Repeated Thanks

"I will give repeated thanks to the Lord, praising Him to everyone. For He stands beside the needy, ready to save them..." Psalm 109:30-31 NLT

When my husband, Joe, took his car for regular maintenance recently, he was hit with an unexpected bill that caused him some concern. When he told me about it, I silently prayed, "Lord, this unexpected expense didn't come as a surprise to You. You saw it coming, and I believe that You will provide the funds we need to cover these charges. Please do it in a way that will simply amaze Joe." Over the next few days, enough money came our way from various sources that enabled us to pay those auto expenses with ease. Joe told me, "Look at that – God provided the exact amount we needed to pay that car repair bill!" When I asked Joe if he had remembered to thank God for the awesome way He came through for us, he said that he had. I told him that it's scriptural to thank the Lord more than once for His blessings, and that David the shepherd-king was in the habit of doing this very thing.

David wrote: "I will give repeated thanks to the Lord, praising Him to everyone." (Psalm 109:30 NLT) I have always tried to remember to thank God more than once for each of His gifts, but recently, I have become more serious about it, and I've been praising Him more and more for all the good in my life. And you know what? I've seen Him do some incredible things to help and deliver my loved ones and me in all kinds of situations.

Right after David says that he will give God "repeated thanks," he says: "For He stands beside the needy, ready to save them." (Psalm 109:31 NLT) I have discovered that there is a definite connection between continually praising God, and witnessing Him move mightily on our behalf. I encourage you to begin giving the Lord "repeated thanks" for all the good in your own life, and watch Him give you more and more to thank and praise Him for!

Lord, forgive me when I have demonstrated a lack of gratitude. Give me a truly thankful heart, and teach me how to give continual thanks to You. Remind me often of all the good in my life, including all of the loved ones You have blessed me with. Fill me with such a profound attitude of gratitude that it will draw others to You through me. Thank You that as I follow Your will in this area, I will have more and more to thank You for!

Promise-Power Point: *God's will for me is to live a life of thankfulness and gratitude toward Him, and as I please Him in this way, I will reap more and more blessings that will reveal to others just how good and generous He really is.*

When We 'Miss' God

"But this one thing I do, forgetting those things which are behind, and reaching forth unto those things which are before, I press toward the mark for the prize of the high calling of God in Christ Jesus." Philippians 3:13-14 KJV

When a young woman wrote me about struggling with feelings of guilt and condemnation because of a decision she had made, she shared with me how she had been faced with two career opportunities. One was so extraordinary that almost everyone she spoke to about it said that she would be crazy not to take it. The other was more ordinary and less impressive in the eyes of her friends and loved ones. Since the first job involved unique and extensive ministry opportunities, this woman felt sure in her heart that this was the path the Lord wanted her to take. Nevertheless, after much prayer and soul searching, she decided to accept the more ordinary opportunity. Though she thoroughly enjoyed her new job, she was plagued with feelings that she had "missed" God, and she began feeling more and more distant from Him. While she admitted that the Lord was still speaking to her through the Scriptures, and still blessing her in many ways, she couldn't deny that her feelings of guilt and condemnation were filling her with fear and doubt.

I told this young woman that I wasn't at all convinced that she missed God by turning down the opportunity that she did. Just because the people around her considered it too good to pass up, that didn't mean that it was the Lord's best for her. She obviously didn't have peace in her heart about doing it, and going against that peace could very well have resulted in devastating results. I told her that there have been many times when I made decisions based on what other people thought I should do – even though I lacked an inner peace about it – and wound up in a place where I never belonged. One such time was years ago when I was presented with the opportunity to work in the office of a successful attorney. Everyone told me that this was a job that could open doors for me. Instead of heeding the lack of peace in my heart, I took the job. From the very first day, I knew I had made a mistake. I was miserable, and I dreaded going to work every day. After only a few weeks, I left that job, feeling guilty about wasting my boss's time and energy, as well as my own.

So what if the young woman who wrote me really had missed God? I told her that if this was the case, it wasn't the end of the world. She should stop letting her fears and regrets haunt her, and she should lay them at the Lord's feet and leave them there. Then she would be more able to serve Him with all of her heart, instead of letting her misgivings steal her energy and her destiny. The truth is that we can't make progress as long as we are dragging regrets behind us. This kind of guilt will weigh us down and keep us from moving forward. It will affect our relationships with others, as well as with God Himself. The devil knows this, and that's why he spends so much time trying to make us feel guilty and condemned.

Do you feel as though you have missed God's will for your life in some respect? Please know that the Lord can give you a fresh beginning. Even if you missed out on God's "Plan A" for your life, rest assured that He has a "Plan B" waiting in the wings for you – a plan that can be just as bright and beautiful as His original one for you. Why? Because He sees your heart, and He knows how much you love Him and want to please Him. In the Book of Nehemiah, when God's laws were read publicly, the people began to weep because they realized how far they were from obeying them. Nehemiah gives them an interesting command. He tells them, "Be not grieved and depressed, for the joy of the Lord is your strength and stronghold." (Nehemiah 8:10 AMP) Beating ourselves up over the mistakes we've made – or think we've made – can weaken us and make us ineffective for God. Don't spend another moment wallowing in guilt and regret. Instead, lay your burden down at the foot of the Cross, and lay hold of the bright future that God has for you!

Lord, give me the wisdom and discernment I need to walk in Your perfect will in every area of my life. Help me not to be led by people, but to always be led by Your Spirit. Thank You that You are greater than my mistakes, and You will lead me in the paths of Your greatest blessings as I trust in You!

Promise-Power Point: *When I choose not to live in fear of making mistakes, and when I do my best to seek and follow God with all my heart, He will direct and re-direct my steps as necessary, so that I can walk in His good plans and purposes for me.*

The Rewards of Childlike Faith

"Let the children come to Me. Don't stop them! For the Kingdom of God belongs to such as these. I assure you, anyone who doesn't have their kind of faith will never get into the Kingdom of God." Mark 10:14-15 NLT

I can still remember when the Lord began teaching me years ago about the blessed rewards of having childlike faith. My husband, Joe, had just lost out on a job that he desperately wanted. When I saw how deeply disappointed he was, I suggested that we ask the Lord to provide another position just like it. To say the least, he wasn't very receptive to my idea. He shot back with comments like, "That was the only job of its kind in that company!" and, "You know nothing about the business world!" I couldn't exactly argue with him. I didn't know much about my husband's line of work, the company he had interviewed with, or the business world, in general. I had been a stay-at-home mom for almost two decades, and I knew very little about "Corporate America". But I knew my God, and I believed that He was always eager to get involved with the little details of our lives whenever we invited Him to. So I began to earnestly pray that the Lord would open up a new door of opportunity for my husband that would not only radically bless him, but that would help him to see our God in fresh, new ways. The Lord did provide an identical job for Joe, and no one was more surprised than he was.

As much as my husband enjoyed his new job, he was very unhappy with his new office. He had always had offices that were bright, cheery, and roomy, and this one was dark, dreary, and cramped. Not only that, but he had to share it with a coworker he was not fond of. When I suggested to Joe that we pray for the Lord to provide him with a new office of his own that would exceed his highest expectations, he said things like, "That's not going to happen! We just had a budget meeting, and there is no money available for anything extra. Besides that, they'd have to make major renovations to our building, and there's no way they would do that now!" I had no doubts that everything my husband said was true, but I couldn't help thinking about the Bible verse that says, "You have not, because you ask not," and I was determined to ask. (James 4:2) Shortly after I began praying for my husband's new office, Joe came home from work one day, and described to me how his company was making major renovations to his building. In wide-eyed amazement, he told me that he was getting a new office that was more than twice the size of his old one, and he wouldn't have to share it with anyone else. Best of all, it would always have plenty of light, because an entire wall would be windows!

Jesus said, "I tell you the truth, anyone who will not receive the kingdom of God like a little child will never enter it." (Mark 10:15 NIV) Not only is childlike faith required for us to enter God's kingdom, but it is also necessary for us to receive many of the blessings the Lord longs to bestow on us in this life. For many years, I was a doubtful, skeptical, and cynical Christian, so I can relate to believers who have a hard time believing in the goodness of God. But I can also relate to believers who have entered into such a deeply personal relationship with the Lord that they have a greater understanding of how eager He is to bless His people. What made the difference? I got to know the true character of God, as revealed in His written Word, the Bible. Spend enough time in the Scriptures, and I guarantee that your faith will grow, and you will have more confidence to ask the Lord for blessings of every shape and size.

I have learned that the Lord is moved by our faith, even on behalf of others. One example of this is in Matthew 9:2, where Jesus heals a paralytic in response to the faith of the man's friends. It's true that my husband didn't have the faith to ask for his own blessings. But it's also true that when he witnessed the Lord's answer to my prayers, it strengthened his faith for the future. What rewards, promotions, and blessings might you be missing out on because you have neglected to ask for them? May the Savior's loving invitation give you a holy nudge today – "Ask, using My name, and you will receive, and your cup of joy will overflow"! (John 16:24 TLB)

Lord, please forgive me for my lack of faith, my doubts, and my cynicism. Give me the heart and the faith of a child, and help me to believe You for all the good things You desire to give me. Show me how to put my faith to work on behalf of others. Help me to feed on Your Word regularly so that my faith will grow. Thank You that Your answers to my prayers will be a powerful testimony to others of Your love and grace!

Promise-Power Point: As I resist all doubt, unbelief, and cynicism – and as I choose as an act of my will to believe in God's matchless goodness and power – I will witness Him performing miracles for me and mine.

Speedy Answers

"For He will finish the work and cut it short in righteousness, because the Lord will make a short work upon the earth." Romans 9:28 NKJV

When our children were 9 and 12 years old, my husband and I decided to move out-of-state. The area we lived in had been steadily going downhill, and because of that, there were hundreds of homes for sale in and around our neighborhood. Our realtor told us to not to expect a quick sale, so we put our house on the market and prepared for a long wait. Amazingly enough, within the first few weeks, we had three bids on our home, and we soon signed a contract with the new buyer. The only problem was that we needed another place to live right away, so we began looking in earnest for a new home. We told our realtor that we needed a vacant house in move-in condition. Considering our time constraints and our financial situation, we knew this would take a miracle, and we prayed for one. We were delighted when we found the perfect vacant home in a lovely area, and we put a bid on it immediately. After waiting several days, we found out that we lost the house to another buyer. Our hearts were heavy with disappointment, and we began to consider less desirable options, such as moving to a hotel or apartment, and putting our furniture and possessions in storage. I fell to my knees in prayer, and

I pleaded with God to move supernaturally to provide us with a wonderful new home without delay. Within the next few days, we found a beautiful house that was vacant and in move-in condition, and in a very desirable area. And we found out later on that we were the talk of realtors for miles around when we were able to secure a mortgage, buy a new home, and move into it in only nine days.

The Bible says, "For He will finish the work and cut it short in righteousness, because the Lord will make a short work upon the earth." (Romans 9:28 NKJV) According to Scripture, there are times when God will supernaturally speed up the work He is doing on this earth. I have seen Him do this in my own life, sometimes as a result of my asking Him to do so. Other times, I have been caught totally off guard when He has moved suddenly in ways I never dreamed possible.

The Bible reveals that God's people often asked for speedy answers to their prayers. Psalm 102:1-2 (TLB) says: "Lord, hear my prayer! Listen to my plea! Don't turn away from me in this time of my distress. Bend down Your ear and give me speedy answers." And David the shepherd-king wrote: "Bow down Your ear to me, deliver me speedily!" (Psalm 31:2 AMP) Scriptures like these give me the confidence to pray for speedy answers from God when I have urgent needs. When I have needed healing in my body, I have often claimed God's promise in Isaiah 58:8 (NKJV): "Your healing shall spring forth speedily." And when I've needed divine protection or deliverance, I have stood on Jesus' promise in Luke 18:8 (AMP): "I tell you, He will defend and protect and avenge them speedily."

I especially like the NASB translation of Romans 9:28, which says: "For the Lord will execute His Word on the earth, thoroughly and quickly." There are times when we will cling in faith to a promise from God, and He will supernaturally accelerate the fulfillment of His Word. Often, the Lord is more than willing to show Himself strong on our behalf in a situation, but He will wait for us to ask Him to do the impossible before He will manifest His miracle-working power.

Yes, there are many times when the Lord will ask us to be still, and to wait patiently for His intervention in a matter. But when we are in desperate need, our God will not fault us for asking Him for speedy help and relief. And just like David, we can cry out, "O answer me speedily!" (Psalm 69:17 AMP)

Lord, when I have urgent needs, give me the faith I need to pray bold prayers. Remind me to ask You to speed up the answers when it would please and glorify You. Guard me from the doubt and unbelief that would rob me of Your best. Thank You for the lives and circumstances that will be changed when You manifest Your miracle-working power on my behalf!

Promise-Power Point: God has the ability and power to speed up answers and events on my behalf, and He will do exactly that when it is His will, and I ask Him to in faith.

The Proper Perspective

"Do not love the world or the things in the world. If anyone loves the world, the love of the Father is not in him." 1 John 2:15 NKJV

My husband, Joe, called me from work one day and asked, "Are you sitting down?" Once I situated myself in a nearby chair, my husband began describing to me how he had parked his car at work as usual, and less than an hour later, it had caught on fire. Joe's company promptly called the fire department, and it took several firefighters to extinguish the fire. People stood around the scene in amazement. Then they began coming up to Joe and saying things like, "I'm so sorry about your car. What are you going to do?" People he had never even met before were offering my husband their condolences. And he found himself saying over and over, "It's only a car. It could have been a lot worse."
Joe couldn't help thinking about the heart attack that almost killed him just two years previous. Since then, his priorities have changed, and as much as he had liked and appreciated his car, he tried to keep things in the proper perspective. He thanked God that he wasn't in the car when it caught fire. And he was grateful that his car wasn't parked in our garage at the time. We could have lost two cars and our house, and we could have been asleep at the time.

Joe's attitude was an inspiration to all of us. Part of me wanted to cry buckets of tears, because we had just applied for a debt consolidation loan earlier that week, and losing Joe's car – which was the best car we had – seemed like a tremendous setback to me. But after we earnestly prayed about it, and sought the Lord daily for His wisdom and guidance, we realized that this series of events was actually for our benefit. God worked miraculously to enable Joe and me to buy a brand new car without it being a hardship for us. I believe that my husband's godly perspective on this calamity paved the way for the Lord to move mightily on our behalf. Scripture says: "He who is of a greedy spirit stirs up strife, but he who puts his trust in the Lord shall be enriched and blessed." (Proverbs 28:25 AMP) When disaster struck, Joe immediately chose to put his trust in God, instead of becoming angry or bitter, or demonstrating a materialistic attitude – and the Lord richly rewarded him for it.

I should have been ecstatic about my husband getting a new car, and for the most part, I was. Unfortunately, there was a part of me that was a little envious. My own car was 19 years old at the time, and while it had served me well, it was finally beginning to show some serious wear and tear. Right after Joe got his new car, I was coming out of the dentist's office – and feeling more than a little downhearted and sore – when I spotted my car from across the street. Paint had started peeling off in some places, and rust had begun to appear. Tears sprang to my eyes and ran down my cheeks as I walked across the street and got into my car. Self-pity overwhelmed me, and I began to pour my heart out to the Lord, confessing my envy, and my desires for a new car of my own. As ashamed and guilty as I felt, I knew that it was important for me to be honest with God. I repented for my wrong attitudes, and I asked Him to help me to be genuinely happy for my husband, and to resist feeling jealous in the future. I thanked Him with all my heart for my old car, and for how it had blessed me and my family, as well as many others. And I told Him that I would not do anything foolish, but would wait on Him until He was ready to provide me with a new vehicle.

It was then that the Lord reminded me of how He had revealed Himself to me in tender ways through this old car throughout the years. When the air conditioner had started malfunctioning, I asked the Lord to fix it for me, knowing full well that my husband was not about to pay to have it repaired. And He had kept it going for me all the years we had it. Time and time again, the Lord revealed His tender loving care through this car, and as I thought about it, I realized that I would not have missed out on those precious moments for anything in the world. I'm reminded of David's words in Psalm 18: "You give me Your shield of victory, and Your right hand sustains me; You stoop down to make me great."
(Psalm 18:35 NIV) If we will call upon the Lord in our times of need, even in the most trivial matters, He will

"stoop down" to bless us, and to show us that He cares. What part of your life could use a touch from God today?

Lord, forgive me for the times I put too much value on the things of this world. Please change my heart, and reorder my priorities, so that they will reflect Your values. Teach me how to be truly happy for others when they are blessed. Thank You that as I turn to You in trouble and expect You to act on my behalf, You will stoop down and touch my life in miraculous ways!

Promise-Powered Point: As I keep a proper, godly perspective in every situation no matter what comes my way, I will experience the Lord revealing His presence and His power on my behalf in extraordinary ways.

Giving God Control

"Unto You, O Lord, do I bring my life." Psalm 25:1 AMP

My husband, Joe, and I were having a heart-to-heart discussion at the dinner table recently, when he told me, "Sometimes I feel like I've been on the wrong path all these years. But if that's true, how do I get on the right path?" I must admit that my husband's heartfelt confession startled me a little. I knew that he had a sincere love for God, but I also knew that he was a bit of a "control freak," and that he regularly struggled with submitting himself to the Lord's will for his life. Making a confession like this one couldn't have been easy for him, and my heart went out to him.

I have met a lot of Christians who are reluctant to give God complete control of their lives, and I sympathize with them. I was almost 40 years old before I truly surrendered my own life to the Lord. I had been a Christian for as long as I could remember, and I trusted Christ enough to get me to heaven, but not enough to become all that He created me to be. Fortunately, I eventually got so weary of trying to manage and control my own life, that I was actually relieved to hand it over to God. When I did, I began to experience the joyful, fruitful, abundant life that Jesus spoke of in the Scriptures. (John 10:10; John 15:1-8)

Why are some believers so afraid of totally surrendering their lives to the Lord? Some of them are afraid that God will make them do things that they despise. But that's completely unscriptural. The Bible says, "Delight yourself in the Lord and He will give you the desires of your heart." (Psalm 37:4 NIV) It doesn't say that if we delight ourselves in the Lord – if we live our lives for Him, and for His purposes – He will make us miserable. Yet many Christians live as though they believe this very thing. They don't realize that many of the dreams and desires that are in their hearts were planted there by God Himself, and that He is even more eager to see them come to pass than they are. And if they would only hand the "reins" of their lives over to Him, He would be more than happy to prove it to them.

Some people are reluctant to give God control of their lives because they don't really believe that His plans for them are actually better than their own. But the truth is that the Lord created us with specific plans and purposes in mind, and there is simply no way we could improve upon them. I like the way one godly man put it: "God will choose for you what you would choose for yourself, if you had enough sense to choose it!"

Scripture says: "'For I know the plans I have for you,' declares the Lord, 'plans to prosper you and not to harm you, plans to give you hope and a future.'" (Jeremiah 29:11 NIV) God wants us to know that His plans for us are good plans. And we will begin to see them unfold as soon as we put aside our own agendas, and submit to His.

A misconception of God can keep some people from surrendering their lives to the Lord. They may think that God only wants to use them for His own selfish purposes, and that He doesn't really want what is best for them. But why would a God who sacrificed His only Son for us – so that He could have an intimate, eternal relationship with us – want to give us anything but the very best? As the Bible says: "Since He did not spare even His own Son for us but gave Him up for us all, won't He also surely give us everything else?" (Romans 8:32 TLB)

That day at the dinner table, I told my husband that if he really wanted to get in on the good plans that God had in store for Him, then he needed to trust the Lord enough to surrender control of his life to Him. If you are in a similar place today, I urge you not to wait another moment. Surrender all that you are and all that you have to the Lord, and begin to live the life of adventure and abundance that belongs to you in Christ!

Lord, I confess that I am tired of being in control of my life. Today, I surrender my whole self to You, and I ask that You help me to fulfill my God-given purpose and potential. Teach me how to do my part by seeking Your guidance and grace daily through prayer and the reading of Your Word. Thank You that Your promise is true – "No eye has seen, no ear has heard, no mind has conceived what God has prepared for those who love Him"! (1 Corinthians 2:9 NIV)

Promise-Power Point: God created me with specific plans and purposes in mind, and I will begin to walk in them when I put my fears and my agenda aside, and align my will with His.

Lessons from Jehoshaphat

"So they turned to attack him, but Jehoshaphat cried out, and the Lord helped him." 2 Chronicles 18:31 NIV

Ever since I began studying the Scriptures years ago, I have been inspired by the life of Jehoshaphat, one of the ancient kings of Judah. He was basically a very good king, but the Bible tells us plainly that he was far from perfect. Even so, the Lord blessed him and used him mightily. Second Chronicles Chapter 20 gives us a glimpse of how this man of God responded in times of trouble. When Jehoshaphat was told that a "vast army" was coming against him, the first thing he did was "resolve to inquire of the Lord." (2 Chronicles 20:2-3 NIV) When you are faced with trouble, do you run to the throne or the phone? One way we can determine our spiritual maturity is by observing who we turn to first when trouble hits.

The next verse in this passage says that, "The people of Judah came together to seek help from the Lord." (2 Chronicles 20:4 NIV) Not only did this king make seeking the Lord Himself a priority, but he got others to join with him in prayer. Jesus spoke of the awesome power available to believers who come together in prayer. He said, "I tell you that if two of you on earth agree about anything you ask for, it will be done for you by My Father in heaven." (Matthew 18:19 NIV) I am blessed with a praying family. And I am always amazed at how we have "come together" in prayer, even at a distance, when trouble has come our way.

As the enemy is bearing down on Jehoshaphat, he pours his heart out to God, declaring his confidence in the Lord's ability and willingness to deliver His people. He says: "If calamity comes upon us, whether the sword of judgment, or plague or famine, we will stand in Your presence before this temple that bears Your Name and will cry out to You in our distress, and You will hear us and save us." (2 Chronicles 20:9 NIV) The most encouraging aspect of this verse for me is that even though God's people may have brought this calamity upon themselves – the "sword of judgment" – Jehoshaphat does not hesitate to ask the Lord for assistance and mercy. If we go back and read Chapter 18, we discover why. Jehoshaphat had previously made an unholy alliance that led him into a trap which almost cost him his life. Scripture tells us that in the heat of battle, "Jehoshaphat cried out, and the Lord helped him." (2 Chronicles 18:31 NIV) Even if our trials are the result of our own stupidity and sin, we can cry out to God for help, and He will hear us. The Lord may not erase all of the natural consequences of our disobedience, but if we will call on Him, He will make His presence known in the midst of our trouble. As King David wrote: "He does not treat us as our sins deserve, or repay us according to our iniquities." (Psalm 103:10 NIV)

The Bible tells us that these enemies coming against

Jehoshaphat and his people are some of the same ones that the Israelites spared when they originally conquered the Promised Land. Jehoshaphat doesn't hesitate to point this out to God in his prayer. He says: "But now here are men from Ammon, Moab and Mount Seir, whose territory You would not allow Israel to invade when they came from Egypt; so they turned away from them and did not destroy them. See how they are repaying us by coming to drive us out of the possession You gave us as an inheritance. O our God, will You not judge them? For we have no power to face this vast army that is attacking us. We do not know what to do, but our eyes are upon You." (2 Chronicles 20:10-12 NIV) God answers Jehoshaphat's prayer for justice by not only giving him and his people the victory, but by rewarding them with "so much plunder that it took three days to collect it." (2 Chronicles 20:25 NIV) When we are kind and merciful to others – especially our enemies – in obedience to God, and they "repay" us with mistreatment, we can ask the Lord to intervene on our behalf and fight our battles for us. As Scripture promises, "We have the Lord our God to help us and to fight our battles for us!" (2 Chronicles 32:8 NLT)

There are many lessons that we can learn from the life of King Jehoshaphat – including the importance of prayer and prayer support, the availability of grace for the guilty, and the rewards of fighting battles God's way. May the Lord plant these principles deep in your heart, so that you may apply them for your good and His glory!

Lord, whenever I am faced with hurt or heartache, remind me to turn to You first. Show me who to seek out for prayer support in every situation and circumstance. Help me to never hesitate to turn to You when my trouble is caused by my own disobedience and foolishness. Thank You that as I depend on You to fight my battles, I will experience the prosperity, security, and victory that belong to me in Christ!

Promise-Power Point: When I decide to shun pride and self-reliance in times of trouble, and I turn to the Lord in humble dependence upon Him, He will fight my battles and give me the upper hand in the end.

About the Author

Since 1998, **J. M. Farro** has served as the devotional writer and prayer counselor for Jesusfreakhideout.com – one of the first and largest Christian music web sites in the world. Her mission is to help others to discover the life-changing power of having a deeply personal relationship with Christ.

Through devotionals, podcasts, blogs, and books – including the best-selling *Life on Purpose* devotional book series – she encourages others to fulfill their God-given purpose and potential. She and her husband, Joe, have two sons, and live in Nazareth, Pennsylvania.

J. M. Farro
P.O. Box 434
Nazareth, PA 18064

jmf@jmfarro.com
farro@jesusfreakhideout.com

www.jmfarro.com
www.jesusfreakhideout.com
www.littlejesusfreaks.com

NOTES

NOTES

Made in the USA
Lexington, KY
09 December 2015